Where Then O Bliss

By
Gary Wilson

Where Then O Bliss

By Gary Wilson

www.garywilson.ca

ISBN-13: 978-0-9784992-9-7

Table of Contents

Part One

GARY WILSON

Chapter 1

Where then, O bliss, is thy balm?

Where, O rapture, thine infinite?

Allen Bill Pond...

As the sun lies dying at Allen Bill Pond, thoughts of Felicia fill the recess of my mind.

Felicia of the unpronounceable last name. Felicia, Felicia, Felicia...

Actually, her name is Felicja, but it corresponds to Felicia in English. Fay-lee-tsya in her native Poland, Fe-lee-sha over here.

I met Felicia early last year. We were both enrolled in an intensive course of environmental studies. Though we were part of a small group of twenty or so people attending long classes daily, we are both standoffish enough that it took us a few days to introduce ourselves to each other and become acquainted. By the time we did do so, it had already become as clear to her as it was to me that we were kindred spirits.

What is it that identifies a kindred spirit, Reader? As I sit here twirling my pen pondering this, the main thing that seems to stand out is intelligence — intelligence as seen in the eyes and the poise or bearing of a person, intelligence plus a little je ne sais quoi. At least, that's what comes to mind as I think of this in relation to Felicia. I don't recall any specific action or words on her part that revealed her to me any more clearly than did the intelligence and that special something I could see in her eyes and poise. I like to think too that the same applied in regard to her perception of me, but be that as it may. What I do know is that when Felicia saw me spending my time staring out the window rather than paying attention in class, she figured that she had found a kindred spirit; and when she heard me introduce myself to the class by saying my name, pausing, wrinkling my brow and then slowly continuing with, "I can think of all kinds of things about myself that I don't want to tell you, but I'm having trouble coming up with anything I do want to tell you," she knew that she'd found one.

Felicia is beautiful. This is true and necessary, necessary twice over. First, this is a story I'm writing. Never mind the fact that it might be perceived by some as a true story. It is still a story, and in our culture the female lead in a story, be it a book, movie or whatever else, is beautiful. It's one of the failings of our culture.

And secondly, I myself incarnate this same weakness such that
I'm able to love only beautiful women. Try as I might, and
believe me I have tried hard, I am completely unable to arouse
any passion within myself for the plain-Janes of this world, no
matter that they are often the more beautiful in spirit.

That said, let me tell you, Reader, how beautiful Felicia is. She
once told me that Polish girls in general are beautiful. I believe
her. I have no reason to disbelieve her. Felicia is slender and of
medium height. I never saw her with dark hair, even though
that's her natural color. Always when I knew her she was
blonde, sometimes a straw-blonde and sometimes with a hint of
henna. The color of one's hair by no means determines or even
enhances beauty, but when Felicia's visiting mother-in-law was
pressuring her to go back to brunette, I thwarted the matron's
efforts with a single disparaging remark — merely because I did
not want my beautiful girl to change in any way.

Felicia's eyes are the color of the Seine, a soft and serene brown
lightened with flecks of green. I've enjoyed many, many hours
diving into those waters, basking in the subtlety of the main
current, being tickled by the tug of innumerable undercurrents. I
dare say no more — dare think no more — of Felicia's eyes.

Although a picture says a thousand words, the reverse is not true:
A thousand words do not say a picture. This is a pity because it

makes it difficult for me to help you envision Felicia. When she was without a speck of make-up, I found her beautiful in a very Slavic way. I would mention full lips, wide spacing of eyes and prominent cheekbones, for whatever illumination that might cast. Made up, she looks very Euro, very enchantress-mystery-of-kohl; she is the fin-de-siècle answer to, image of, Brigitte Bardot.

Is Felicia a smiler, a sunny personality? Need you ask, Reader?

I knew Felicia to smile but seldom. Her smiles were like gems, rare and precious. I think — rather, I should say that I know — that this was something that drew her to me. I am confused within myself as to what I mean by this: On the one hand, it is true that she perceived me, as it seems does everyone, to be as austere in countenance as I have just described her. She once saw some old photos of me in which I had long blond hair and I was just staring existentially at the camera. She was struck by these photos. She saw herself in them. And she was right. It might as well have been her staring at the camera, thinly disguised, very thinly disguised, by my features. But on the other hand, appearances can be, and in this case are, deceiving, for I am a veritable well of optimism and inner sanguinity. Unlike Felicia, whose solemnity of demeanor is due to a profound sadness, my own is more akin to ennui. So I'm not entirely unconfused as to whether she was drawn to a bird of her own feather, or attracted to an opposite. I suspect that, paradoxically, both are true.

Let me get Jean-Paul and France out of the way right now. No conscious attempt has been made to season the preceding passages along such lines. The simple fact is that Felicia is a true Pole and the heart of every true Pole lives in Paris no matter whether the body resides there too or in Chicago, London or Warsaw itself. For me to think or talk about Felicia completely without reference to things French would be both nonsensical and impossible; it would be like talking about Catherine the Great with no mention of Russia, Cleopatra without Rome, Helen sans Troy — simply preposterous.

Have I given you a fair enough picture of Felicia yet? Are you able to visualize an image that is more personality than anonymity? Can you begin to comprehend her beauty? Now let me tell you the anomaly: Felicia wears glasses. We all know from Hollywood's teaching that a beautiful girl need do nothing more strenuous than donning a pair of glasses to turn herself into a frump, a wallflower ignored by all men. (Didn't Marilyn Monroe, of all people, do this precise thing in one or more of her movies?) And of course we also know what baloney that is, for various reasons. Well, interestingly enough, in Felicia's case this "wallflower effect" is very nearly fully realized. This is because of her lens prescription. When nearsighted people wear glasses, others do not see their eyes to appear magnified; in fact, the opposite is true, but it is only with strong lenses that the eyes appear noticeably shrunken. It is farsighted people who wear glasses that make their eyes appear magnified ("googly-eyed", to use the scientific term); but since most farsighted people wear glasses only while reading (or not at all, for that matter), it's really a small percentage of regular glasses-wearers whose appearance is actually changed very drastically by the donning of glasses. It just so happens, though, that Felicia is one of these. She is farsighted, and worse yet (in this respect), farsighted in only one eye. When she was a child growing up in Poland, she had a severe bout with one of the childhood diseases. Due to the lack there at the time of the appropriate medication, she almost lost her young life, but ended up pulling through. This affliction left its mark on her, though, in the form of a scarred retina in one eye. Imagine, then, our Felicia having just put on her glasses as described. It really does not matter, does it, how beautiful she is? She has effectively concealed her beauty and transformed herself into the proverbial wallflower.

Chapter 2

Felicia and I spent forty hours per week in class. Upon discovering each other, that occurring a few days after our studies commenced, we spent forty hours per week together. Together.

The instantaneity of the depth and breadth of the bond between Felicia and me is a thing of amazement. I don't say that I stand in wonder of it, but only because to me our friendship was the most natural thing in the world. Yet to any perspective other than mine or hers it must seem completely unfathomable. We were from different cultures. We were raised in different, and adversarial, ideological regimes. If you consider Catholicism and Protestantism to be different religions, and we did, we were from different religions, and both devoutly so in our different ways. And most importantly, we were both deeply imbued with a sense of the inviolability of marriage which, applied in our particular situation, can be taken to mean the inviolability of Felicia's marriage. How then, particularly in light of the last, could such an intimacy develop between the two of us, and so swiftly? I have reflected on this a lot. When I say "reflected", I could just as well say "twisted, wiggled and wormed" because in trying to reconcile this blatant violation of propriety with my own deeply-ingrained sense of morality it more often feels like I am trying to worm myself out of self-condemnation than merely reflecting on the matter. There's a lot of truth to this, on the one hand, yet it's a complete misrepresentation of the underlying reality on the other. It is all a matter of perspective. In the eyes of the world, Felicia and I were in blatant violation of society's precepts, yet from our own uniquely-informed perspective our path was not only one of innocence, but even one, exclusively so, of rightness. This is possible, and true, because of Felicia's marital status. Although legally, and thus to the world, she was a married woman, in the deeper realm of life, on the spiritual plane, Felicia was as free and as unbound as any virgin bride-to-be. I give you my oath that in the eyes of God — and no others matter — Felicia was free to love and be loved. But I don't want to get ahead of the story.

Having an idea of Felicia's reticence, you will not be surprised that for quite some time, though knowing her, I knew next to nothing of her. Here, for instance, is an amusing example: How old was Felicia? Had Woman not already made age an eternal mystery, She would have learned it at Felicia's knee. My best guess, incorrect as I learned, was that Felicia was two years younger than me. How did I find out the truth? To what indignity did I subject my self-respect to satisfy my curiosity? None, actually. It was funny how it came about. One day in February my Silesian sphinx held out her driver's license to show me how unlike the bespectacled photo was her own dear self, dear bespectacled self. It was my assumption that the real intent was the discreet communication of age, and accordingly, I glanced at the birth date and in reciprocal discretion kept my mouth shut. It was only later, a few days or weeks down the road, that I — we — learned that Felicia had slipped. She playfully asked me one day to guess her birthday and I quizzically looked at her and said, "But it's June 12!" And the expression on my face was, "Duuuhh! Do you think I'm stupid or something?" I can still see her outrage, very feminine, tempered by love and subsiding in a blush of self-reproach as I revealed my source of intelligence and exposed the traitor in our midst.

I was always honest and candid with Felicia, perfectly so. If she asked a question, I gave her the answer. If the answer reflected poorly on me, I gave it to her. If the answer reflected well on me, I gave it to her. My candor and honesty were constant. I satisfied her every curiosity. On occasion she called me shameless. She was correct. I was shameless. To this day I remain so. That said, there is something unexpected about candor, such candor or any candor. In the end it raises just as many questions as reticence, and so in a sense is just as mysterious. It's ironic.

Forty hours a week together like we were manacled, that's how Felicia and I were. The other people studying with us were good people and interesting to varying degrees, but we were interested

11

only in each other. We sat and whispered and wrote notes back and forth all day long like a couple of twelve-year-olds. Très juvenile. Have you ever experienced such proximity to anyone? There's a getting-to-know someone that's entirely nonverbal, and this is far more intimate than the words we exchange which are just a hash and rehash day after day of the same old nothingness. There is a lot of wisdom to that old Greek philosopher who became so disenchanted with it all that the only sincere response left for him was to wag his finger and shake his head.

Our day together usually began at eight o'clock when class commenced. At first we both took the LRT — public transit — to school, then after a few weeks I drove instead. I say "eight o'clock", but as I'm sure you already realize without me having told you, Felicia was seldom on time. How could she be? She was Felicia. When she did arrive and get settled in, she would start the day with Question Number One: "Chimney kohash?" To which I would rightly reply, "Koham." That, as you've guessed already, is the Polish tongue rendered into easy-reading English and I will not insult your intelligence by making the obvious translation. For the next four hours our classmates would faithfully drink in and scribble down the words of the various Solons who deigned to grace us with their instruction. Felicia too was a conscientious note-taker, and I found this frightfully annoying on those not infrequent occasions when I had some pressing bit of conversation to make only to find her attention anything but undivided. However, we all have our failings and there was a certain charm in Felicia's scholastic concern.

Throughout the morning there were a couple short breaks to stretch our legs and then at noon we had close to an hour for lunch. When Felicia saw me in the first few days of school bring nothing or a few pieces of fruit for lunch, she took pity on me and fretted that I was going to waste away to skin and bone. You should have seen the meals she was packing to school. They give the word "bag-lunch" a whole new meaning. I swear there was never a day on which she brought less than four courses, all prepared of such quality that, given a plate and appropriate cutlery, they could have been served in any self-respecting French restaurant. You can see why I had difficulty turning down her generosity. I did try to explain to her that, being a bachelor, I had discovered how I could get proper nutrition by eating a huge bowl of granola for breakfast, next to nothing for lunch and the unavoidable prepared meal for supper, and in this way greatly minimize the amount of effort expended in both making meals and cleaning all the dishes, cookware and utensils involved. But my protests, which started out half-hearted in the first place, soon enough withered away entirely. Instead, I repaid Felicia by spending our lunch hours working with her on her English. I know, Reader — this sounds like nothing more than a pretext. In my own defense I can point out that I have received formal education in linguistics and my fascination with the field is deep enough to qualify me as a lay linguist at least. Even had I not been interested in Felicia, I would have been happy to work with her in this area. All the same, it was something of a pretext. Had we spent our lunch hours together in more chitchat, they would have become stale and listless. Having a genuine purpose lifted them from such a prospect and gave them vibrancy; not to mention the fact that proper linguistic assistance can and should be quite intimate.

We would eat lunch in the classroom and then go for a stroll, sometimes in the immediate hallway and sometimes further afield. If the weather allowed it, we liked to go outside. Eventually we would find some private spot to stop at and practice English. There are some very nice gardens at SAIT where we could happily lose ourselves for the whole noon-break once the weather had become warmer. There is something in nature that gives a heightened poignancy to love. Whether indoors or out, our love for one another was equally profound, but in those memories where I can see us lolling under the blue, blue sky, shaded by elms and willows, and wafted by the fragrance of lilies, carnations and gladiolas, the passion of it comes back to me so much more piercingly.

We often returned to class late after lunch, sometimes rather out of breath for hurrying back. I have already described our classmates as good people. For the most part — that is to say, for most of them — this is entirely true. However, there was more than one who now and then felt that special crusader call to assert themselves in defense of public morality. Oh, the looks we would get from these! As a guy, I can only wish that Felicia and I had done even half of what their accusatory glances had already convicted us of.

Afternoons were about the same as mornings. It must have been four o'clock when classes would finish each day. At first Felicia and I took the LRT home together. She lived a few miles further on the same line I lived on. I don't remember why I would have gotten a bus pass in the first place rather than just driving, because I'm really not a public transportation sort of person. Anyway, I did use the LRT through January and then always after that I drove. Felicia still came to school on the LRT, but we left together in my car. With the extra time this made available, we would either go shopping or repair to my lair. We never had a lot of time, half or three-quarters of an hour at the most, but this was the most precious of the day. Privacy. No distractions. No agents of righteousness. No chance encounters. Why is Time so perverse? Why must it fly so fast when the children of earth have found for themselves these fleeting bits of heaven with which to mask the nothingness? The only greater tragedy we could have felt than parting each day, a tragedy fully reborn and experienced anew day by day by day, would have been to have not been together at all.

I always dropped Felicia off at the bus stop where she would have gotten off to walk home. Then the day was over. It was seldom that she would telephone me, and I of course never called her.

Chapter 3

It's interesting to observe the motives that drive those who put their noses into other people's business. There were two such people among our fellow students, one female and one male, and yes, Reader, you guessed it — the one had early on been spurned by me and the other at about the same time by Felicia. Why the two of them did not just slink off the field, lick their wounds and mind their own business beats me. As it turned out, although they really had little enough in common, their mutual opposition to the relationship between Felicia and me caused them to join forces and end up, if I'm not mistaken, becoming quite close themselves. At least, they certainly ended up working together closely to spite us.

The female was an alpha type. She had a pretty face and was spoiled, petulant and aggressive. Annoying, very annoying. She was like a brunette version of Nellie Olson off of 'Little House on the Prairie'. However, unlike the heartless-yet-divine Nellie, this alpha had the misfortune to have a Big Bird physique that put her irrevocably beyond the pale, beyond my pale at any rate.

The male was a yoga-propagating, acoustic guitar-playing, Kumbaya-singing, Neanderthal-boned freak with a face like a

Spiderman villain (the one named Rhino-man, to be precise).
There was no backhanded compliment to me whatsoever in
Felicia's preference of myself over him. She viewed him as
something of a monster. He had a way of hovering on the
periphery of her vicinity and she came to dread even the slightest
communication with him.

Other than hovering, in their two different ways, these creatures
really did not actually bother us in the first two or three months.
If they'd just held themselves on an even keel and kept their
feelings toward us from degenerating into such malignancy, they
never would have come to make such fools of themselves.

For quite a while, there was nothing palpable to alert Felicia or
me that anything was brewing, but gradually an undercurrent
began to develop that foreshadowed trouble of some degree. We
could never hear, were never subjected outright to, the gossip
that was going on about us, yet its silent echoes grew ever more
clearly etched in the eyes and faces of these good people
studying with us. There were different responses. Some just did
not care one way or another, and were totally unaffected. Some
carefully avoided the temptation to be busybodies, and made a
point of treating us as they naturally would, perhaps even
indulging us a little as one indulges those whom one is making a
conscious effort at not being biased against. Some let their
disapproval show in a slight cooling toward us. And some

wavered, not having any real inclination to intrude, yet obviously being influenced by the idle chatter. The thing was that there was really nothing anyone could say to us. It is true that we were shameless in our intimacy in front of them, even if we did have enough discretion to observe the dictates of decorum. Yet we caused no one any harm; we were just doing our own thing in our own little world. It was this, in fact, ironically enough, that was the true, underlying cause of any resentment felt toward us by some of our fellow students — with the exception of our two special friends. We were having fun, a lot of fun, while everyone else was just slogging along in the drudgery of the studies; and worse yet, we were not bonding with the rest of the group — and this was taken, even if not meant, as rejection.

The first incident revolved around our whispering. Felicia and I sat in the very back of four rows. There was nothing behind us but windows looking west on trees, shrubs, walks and a driveway. We sat four inches apart, no more (ostensibly so I could help her while keeping my voice down). Rhino-man and one or two other students sat in the row directly ahead of us. Nellie Olson was in the front row. Nobody could hear the words of what we were saying ever, and it was seldom that the sound of our whispering was even detectable beyond the nearest few students, other than the odd giggle or other eruption. All the same, we should have been forewarned, and I suppose we were, when all of a sudden our instructors began caring whether or not anyone talked during class and requesting that a dead silence be maintained.

One morning in the end of March, or in April, I arrived at school to find Rhino-man sitting at my desk. Though there was no formal assignment of desks, there was an unwritten proprietorship each of his own respected by all. Sitting like this in my desk and refusing to vacate it when I asked him to move was a serious act of effrontery. Then he had the nerve to pontificate against the whispering between Felicia and me as if it caused injury to the whole class and he spoke for each and every one of our fellow students. My first thought was to pick the sorry beggar up and heave him bodily out of my seat, maybe even pile drive him or toss him through the windows behind us for good measure. However, I stopped to make some quick calculations and realized that pitting my ten-minus stone of scrawn against his fifteen or so of Frankenstein incarnate would be an act more of comedy than prowess. So I resisted the temptation to get physical. I practiced a little French on him instead, but this got us nowhere as he seemed to be unrepentantly unilingual. I remained by my desk. It was a stand-off. I was not budging, and neither was he. Felicia arrived. If Rhino-man thought that she was going to sit at her desk beside him, he was dreaming. She remained standing there with me. She was not sitting by him and she was not sitting elsewhere. By this time the classroom was in a general uproar and the administrator came in to deal with the situation.

When it came time to stand up and be counted, the only people who found our whispering particularly trying were the indefatigable Nellie, who it became obvious had been lobbying the instructors of late to make their calls for classroom silence, and Rhino-man, who believe it or not, had by now discovered in himself a hearing impairment which was aggravated by exposure to whispering. Never mind that Nellie sat at the very front, far enough from us that she would have needed a CIA-style listening device to catch anything we were saying, or that her accomplice with his newfound hearing ailment was placing himself even further from where the instructors stood rather than taking an empty seat up front. It was all quite ridiculous. A few others spoke up to try to find some middle ground, but the affront — both to myself and to Felicia — was so clearly indefensible that the eventual outcome was Rhino-man's surrender of my desk. He looked like a fool.

But that wasn't the conclusion of the episode. The best was yet to come. Felicia called her husband and told him all about how this creature had tried to take my desk and sit beside her, and how the administrator had dragged his heels in chasing the beast back to where he should have been. Her husband already knew that I helped explain things in English to Felicia and that was why we sat together. By the time she finished describing the whole ordeal to him, he was in as great a rage as we were, maybe greater.

I should tell you a little about this administrator, the poor man. He knew that Felicia was married and he had also become aware that she and I were close friends. The problem with him — and innocent it was, I truly believe — was his unsettling habit of popping up at the most inconvenient (or maybe I should say, "easily-misinterpretable") times. He had done this on us twice, and upstanding Calvinist that he was, there was little doubt that Felicia and I were not his favorite people. Nevertheless, to my knowledge he was discreet. Anyhow, when he had to come to the classroom that morning and confront a situation where, on the one side, were ranged one of his trusty informants along with another dependably pliable student, and on the other, but unfortunately in the right, his two shameless, incorrigible miscreants, it was doubtlessly all he could do to force himself to do the right thing. I'm sure that he did sincerely tell himself that it would be in the interests of society in general if Felicia and I were forced apart, so it really was against his better judgment to go and re-establish the old status quo. He likely also felt that he owed Felicia's husband, householder to householder, some sort of effort at disrupting her relationship with me.

Imagine, then, Reader, this poor administrator's sense of shock when Mr. Breadwinner calls him up that afternoon and tears a strip up one side of him and down the other. Felicia's husband, loquacious at the best and worst of times and always in between, talked to him for a full hour going over and over things from all possible perspectives. And from all reports he did not talk — he screamed, not letting his poor old victim get a word in edgewise. If that administrator had had any misgivings about not sticking his nose into our business, after that phone call they were all gone. He had done his due diligence and then some, and he was washing his hands of us and any further thoughts of interfering.

You would think that after going to such lengths to provoke a confrontation, and then seeing their efforts come to naught, we wouldn't have heard another peep out of either of our two nuisances. Wrong! There was a respite, to be sure, but it was just so that they could recharge their batteries and grope around until they found something or other else we were doing wrong that was arguably harmful or contained such potential. And what did they find? Well, let me put it this way: I'm never going to suggest that either Felicia or I would have stooped to cheating on exams. Myself because, being a confirmed dilettante in good standing, I would be mortified to the core to think that anyone could even consider accusing me of ever caring what sort of score I might be awarded in any course or test. Felicia because, as I believe I explained in Chapter Two, she is beautiful. I do not care what anyone else might have thought they saw, nor that, as reported to me by both Felicia and her husband, in her native culture cheating is socially acceptable and perceived along the lines of "group effort"; Felicia would never have dreamed of cheating on any exam whatsoever, both because she was beautiful and because the thought of causing such irreparable injury to our esteemed fellow students would have put her into a state of anguish.

Am I making myself clear, Reader? Have you guessed yet what dastardly new tack our two little friends were taking? Yes, indeed. They had lowered themselves to — Perish the thought! — accusations of examination fraud.

How can I proceed here with the appropriate delicacy? I've already stated that Felicia neither cheated on exams nor considered doing so. Perhaps, then, I can say that there were frequent and widespread misperceptions among our classmates, which she shamelessly disregarded with reckless abandon, that they were observing her in the very act of cheating on tests. It is funny the crazy ideas people get into their heads! Well, this was an ongoing thing and it really must have ground on our Nellie Olson, of all people, to have to sit back and do nothing. The problem was that, besides the poor old administrator's obvious reluctance to get within ten-foot-pole range of Felicia, she was pregnant and it would have been exceptionally bad form to have gone after her. There was the odd snide remark from Nellie Olson about cheating along with the equally snide suggestion that the seating order be randomly changed just for tests, but that was all. This state of affairs might have lasted through the conclusion of the program, except for a couple tests in which I was the one so maliciously misperceived as to be cheating. This was late May.

Don't even ask, Reader, why I conducted myself so as to allow for the misperception that I was cheating. As if I cared what kind of marks I got! Nevertheless, there you have it. On the second occasion, Rhino-man, alerted, watchful and prepared in strategy, catches me seemingly in delicto flagrante and of course he did have to call out, snitch that he was, and make as big a stink about it as he possibly could. Nothing came of this in itself, nothing that ever discomfited me. However, it did encourage Nellie Olson in her calls for exam-time musical chairs, and give her enough ammunition so that finally she got her wish.

By this time it was June. We did one of these tests and I got an idea. I told Felicia I was going to give her a treat money could not buy for her birthday: I was going to hand our beloved Nellie Olson the come-uppance that for the last five months she had been begging for. Felicia loved the idea.

The next time we had one of these musical chairs tests I casually loitered near the middle of the classroom so as to be within a two-second lunge of any desk in the room. You have to keep in mind that the one and only purpose for the random seating was to split Felicia and me, and so I was free to sit anywhere I liked without threat of calls for a re-seating as long as I was not beside her.

Have you guessed yet what I was up to, Reader? As soon as Nellie took her seat, there I was beside her. Felicia already knew to sit far enough away but with a good view, so she took a seat two rows directly behind me. The test began.

I scribbled away, calmly displaying my aptitude at basket-weaving. But though I was writing, all my attention was focused on my unwitting prey as I waited and prepared for the best moment to pounce. I relaxed. I loosened up. I twiddled with my pencil. I ensured that my test paper was in good view. Nellie did a lot of writing, but she was happily surprised to be sitting beside me and she relaxed too. She loosened up. She twiddled with her pencil. At last she was positioned perfectly, not facing me of course, but angled in my direction. Though not looking directly at me or my paper, her focus was on me. I bent over my paper. Then, with my pencil right over my paper, I flicked it with a funny movement that caught her eye. I could not see her through the back of my head, but I knew it could not but catch her eye. Immediately, I snapped up my head, turned in my chair and shrieked her name in a tone of indignant consternation.

The timing could not have been better if we had been choreographed. I caught the sorry biche square on. She was the proverbial deer in the headlights. She looked guiltier than sin.

Not a word came out of her mouth (for once, amazingly). All she could do was huff and squeak, blushing fiercely all the while and looking around as if she were seeking a place to hide. I glared at her good and hard, then shifted myself in my chair to give her my back and leaned my arm onto the desk for good measure to be certain her view of my test paper was entirely blocked.

Somehow I kept a straight face and finished the test. Keeping my composure was no easy thing, for there was quite a bit of snickering, especially from Felicia who was nearly dying of laughter a few feet behind me, but I did manage it. Felicia had carefully watched the whole thing start to finish and later told me that it could not have played out more perfectly had dear Nellie been practicing for the role. It was indeed a memorable birthday gift for my darling.

GARY WILSON

Chapter 4

Chapter Four, Chapter Four, Chapter Four... A story should be something like life, sometimes humorous, sometimes meditative, sometimes romantic, always of the profoundest integrity. We have now come to the season of bleakness, the desolate winter of our tale. Brace yourself, Reader, for here in Chapter Four you will find no mirth, no poetry, nothing but the wastelands of the soul. You have been warned.

Violence against women. Spousal abuse. Wife-beating. A serpent by any other name is still a serpent. What dysfunction is it in modern man that results in this most repulsive and incomprehensible form of brutality? I like to think of myself as a student of nature. I often look to the animals for wisdom. I say this in a holistic, generalist sense. Humanity is such a maelstrom of change right now that one can hardly glean any sort of guidance out of all its shifts, twistings and reversals. And do you know what I see in the animals? Or should I say, what I don't see? Of all the violence, bloodthirstiness and ruthlessness I see in the animal kingdom, mate abuse is the one brutality I do not see. I've seen cheetahs chase down cute little Thompson's gazelles — Who hasn't? — and quickly gorge on their protein-rich guts and large organs before the hyenas can come and snatch the rest.

I've seen elephants destroying trees just to get at the branches or leaves they want to consume. I've seen house cats playing with their captive prey so as to practice and hone their skill in pouncing. I've seen a mother bird fill her gullet with carrion flesh torn from a day-old animal carcass to take back and regurgitate for the feeding of her young. I've seen a lion defend his territory to the death. And I've seen rams and bulls of untold species fight to various degrees of viciousness just for the right to propagate their genes. But I have never seen a stallion beating his mares. I have never seen a bull beating his cows. I have never seen a boar beating his sows. Nor a cock his hens, a gander his geese, nor any male of any species his mate. Has my nature show viewing been somehow remiss? Is there some long-overlooked, socially significant, dirty little secret here that some quick-witted and enterprising telejournalist can capitalize on? 'Mate Abuse in the Wilds: The Untold Story'? I don't think so. Animals do not beat their mates. The simple fact is that this particular monstrosity is entirely human in its scope. We've invented a million other things. Is it any surprise that we should have originated this as well?

Felicia and Pyotr were married in Poland. He never beat her there. Her first beating came sometime after they'd fled across the Iron Curtain and were living in West Germany. He was remorseful when he was done, and it was only after they had settled in Canada that his beatings became a regular occurrence.

From then on, there was a pattern to Pyotr's beatings of Felicia. They came a month or so apart. Pressure from various frustrations at work would build within him until he was at the point where he would explode. And explode he always did, at her expense. Then he was cool for a while and everything was peachy. When he quit working for a couple years and enrolled in business school, the pressure he felt apparently increased because the beatings throughout that period were more vicious and frequent, but otherwise the general pattern remained the same.

Why did Felicia put up with this? We should ask why any woman puts up with it. I'm no psychologist, but I can point out a few things. First, in a sense it started gradually, increasing; she was eased into it. Secondly, as in any marital relationship, there was a strong bond between Felicia and Pyotr, a great deal of emotional equity. Thirdly, she blamed herself for the beatings, as victims so often do. And fourthly, she was a mother with a young child, responsible not only for her own wellbeing, economic or otherwise, but for that of the child as well. These factors, along with others, I'm sure, are likely to be found in the majority of spousal abuse situations.

Under regular circumstances in our society, spousal abuse is a difficult matter for a woman to deal with, to confront with any confidence that she is pursuing the best path. Our society has not yet found an equilibrium in which it can deal effectively with this scourge. Now consider the fact that Felicia was an immigrant in a strange new land. She did not have a single friend or relative in the entire continent she could go to. She had grown up in a country where the mindset was that the last place you would turn to for help was the government. Her religion taught her submissiveness, longsuffering and the sacredness of marriage over pretty much everything. She was about as emotionally and informationally isolated as any brute could ever hope his victim to be. She could hardly speak a word of English when she got here, for heaven's sake! (And even when I first became acquainted with Felicia, her facility with the language was sorely lacking.) Is it any wonder that, when Pyotr told her that if she ever tried to leave him then he would have her committed to an insane asylum, she believed him? — that if she were ever to divorce him then he would get custody of their child and never let her see him again, she believed that as well? In some societies these things are true. The result is that, although the plight of our own victimized daughters is bad enough, that of our adopted daughters is often many times worse.

Do you understand now, Reader, why I can say that Felicia was free, on a spiritual level, from all bonds of marriage? True marriage is a union of love and produces the fruits of love. Pyotr's possession of Felicia was nothing but the expression of lust, his aim not to cherish and nurture but merely to dominate.

Abuse — and particularly chronic abuse — is no part of love. Felicia was not a married woman. Yes, in the eyes of the law she was bound by marriage. But in the eyes of the deeper reality, such "marriage" carries no standing or significance. The societal convention of marriage is nothing more than an economic contract dressed up in finery. True marriage is the sacrament of love, entirely spiritual in scope, yet manifested in a physical incarnation. When Felicia married Pyotr, she sincerely believed, like any bride, that this spiritual union was what she was entering. She was deceived. She was never so married, which is to say, she was never married at all. When Pyotr showed his true colors and commenced with the abuse, he demonstrated that he had entered the union under false pretenses. His actions annulled their marriage, demonstrated that it had never existed in the first place. That bears repeating with emphasis: Pyotr's chronic abuse of Felicia demonstrated that no true marriage had ever taken place between the two of them. Felicia was a free woman, free to love whom she chose, free to get or not get the legal divorce of a marriage that existed in no other sense.

So far we have considered the matter of spousal abuse from a distant, intellectual perspective. Let me conclude this discussion with a description of one of the worse beatings, perhaps the worst, which Felicia ever received.

It was summertime, the summer before we met. August. In

Calgary, August is one of the most pleasant months. The temperatures are warm and soothing. There is little rain and almost constant sunshine. Being at a high elevation right beside the Rockies, the air becomes cool at night and is very fresh in the morning. If you're going to do a little painting outside, there is no better time for it.

Felicia decided to paint the fence at their home. It was a big job, but she was up to it. There was not the slightest question of Pyotr assisting her in any way. That was just not something he would do. She tackled the task and over a period of a few days got it done. But right at the end, while she was on a ladder reaching a little too far to do some touch-ups, she fell and hurt her leg. It was not a serious injury, but it did leave her hobbling along in pain.

Normally, being the last 1950's-style model housewife left on earth, Felicia had a full, twelve-course, steaming-hot evening feast ready on the table when Pyotr returned home after work. On this day, being tired out from all the painting and stiffly limping from her fall, she decided instead to prepare just a simple cold repast. Need I point out that Felicia's "simple cold repast" still involved about twice as much preparation as any self-respecting bachelor's entire week's worth of cuisine? Two salads. Three kinds of sandwiches. Vegetables and dip. Crackers with cheese. Dessert. I guarantee there would have been nothing less than this.

Pyotr was late. Felicia went ahead and ate with her son so she could put him to bed. She covered the dishes and put a couple of them in the fridge to stay cool. After putting the boy to bed, she relaxed in the family room.

Eventually Pyotr got home. Work was bothering him. It had been a while since he had given Felicia a beating. When he stepped into the house, she felt too stiff to get up and wait on him as she usually would have. She told him what to get from the fridge to go with what was on the table. He was displeased to have no hot meal waiting. He told her to come make something hot for him. She refused. She told him that she was in pain and just wanted to rest. This was all too much for Pyotr. He grabbed her by the arm and dragged her into the kitchen ordering her to make a hot meal for him. She refused, pointing out everything that was already prepared. He lost it.

Right there in the kitchen, in spite of her previous injury and screams, Pyotr beat Felicia to within an inch of her life. He slammed her against the walls and cupboards. He beat her with his fists, bloodying her nose and cutting her lip. He knocked her around and around the room until her blood could be found everywhere and on everything, table, chairs, walls, cupboards, fridge, stove, floor and all. He kicked her off her feet and pummeled and kicked her from head to toe, using some of the judo moves that he liked so much to practice. By the time he finished, all Felicia could do was lie there moaning and whimpering. She thought for sure she had internal injuries. She was a mass of bruises and could feel pain over every square inch of her body.

After a regular beating, it would fall to Felicia eventually to clean up the mess. But this time Pyotr realized he may have gone too far. He hustled her upstairs to their bedroom and then carefully scrubbed away the blood from all over the kitchen. When Felicia looked at it in the morning, there was no evidence of the previous night's assault. Even the towels Pyotr had used for the clean-up were gone.

Part Two

GARY WILSON

Chapter 5

Let's step back now, Reader, to early January and the
commencement of my friendship with Felicia.

The environmental studies program we were enrolled in was a
government-funded training program. A few months earlier I had
been laid off from my job and for the first and, I'm sure, only
time in my life I collected employment insurance benefits. In the
time-honored Canadian tradition, I continued to work full-time
so that my total income was actually enough to allow me to start
paying off my student loans and other debts. This was going
nicely until at the end of the year I was approaching the cut-off
of my benefits and I still had a ways to go with my debts, besides
which I really wanted to put a little away so that come
springtime I could run off to Europe and spend the summer
traipsing around there in search for whatever mischief and
meaning could be found. I really was desperately bored with
things in Canada.

When I saw these studies being advertised with the promise of
the extension of my benefit payments through the duration, it
seemed like a heaven-sent opportunity. I would get myself
accepted, show up for classes a day or two a week, collect my

income supplement and still fit in a full week's work moonlighting. Big Brother was doing good by me. When April or May rolled around I would be out of debt and have enough money to finance a summer's backpacking getaway.

What I had not anticipated was attendance being required and checked twice daily. I hadn't had my attendance taken or recorded as a student since high school. The thought, even, had grown foreign to me. As you can imagine, this really wreaked havoc with my own program. How was I supposed to get anywhere with my plans when such a huge chunk of my time would be so wastefully occupied? We're talking about a good forty hours a week here, plus travel time to and fro. The pittance this block of time would be earning me — the operative word here being "earning", in contrast to what was before simply "netting" (as my rightful due — my Canadian birthright, no less) — certainly did not justify the loss of its free availability to me. But by the time I learned of this state of affairs, classes had of course already started. I held out hope for a few weeks — and fit as much work as possible into evenings and weekends — until it really did sink in that I was being shafted by my own government. Stabbed in the back. Hung out to dry. Left twisting in the wind. I doubt if such a thing ever happened in Newfoundland, ever really happened there.

I should say a word about that program. I scoffed at it from start to finish, and there was a lot to scoff at, a lot of repetitiveness and fluff for marking time among the nuggets of real value, the various certifications. Yet, looking back, I have to admit in all honesty that it has influenced my outlook, my philosophy, tremendously. The two essential things it enriched me with are an appreciation and respect for the natural environment, along with the accompanying mistrust of technological advances; and a vastly broadened perspective in the approach to system development and maintenance, an awareness of the possible systemic significance of even the tiniest aspects, whether we are talking about a business, a machine, a society, an eco-system, an animal or any other complex whole.

Anyway, as I have mentioned, Felicia and I gravitated toward each other quite early on in the course of these studies. And I have told you, Reader, that my love of linguistics provided the context for our initial interaction. I genuinely wanted to discover what in Felicia's mechanics of pronunciation led her to butcher my beloved English language so extravagantly; at the same time I was more than happy to help her make an effort at improvement.

The interesting thing about Felicia's grasp of English was the technical perfection. I dare say her grammar was better than my own, certainly better than the majority of our classmates. Also, she had a good-sized vocabulary. On paper her ability was far beyond adequate. This is none too unusual. In fact, it is quite typical for those whose language-learning is primarily in the classroom or from self-help books. You can find a million such speakers of English on the campuses across the English-speaking world. Felicia's problem was the actual delivery of the words, the sounds of which the words were composed. She had to work on practically all aspects of both vowel and consonant formation, not to mention stress, rhythm and flow, the latter of which at first I did not even attempt to tackle.

The fact is, to the detriment of Felicia and all other foreign learners of the language, English is quite exotic. The vowel systems of most European languages are relatively similar to each other, and far more similar, generally-speaking, to those of other languages than to ours. Likewise the primary stops: p, t, and k. Our letter r, on which we have the exclusive worldwide patent, is such an oddity (bona fide museum collection material) and such an impossibility to the adult learner that I never even considered wasting my time trying to work with Felicia on it.

We began the whole process in January with me listening carefully and making notes as my patient would read lists of words chosen specifically to illuminate various sounds in different ways. An example of what this showed me is that she could pronounce the letter g just fine if it was at the start, or in the middle, of a word; but if it came at the end of the word she invariably changed it to a k. (For instance, "dog" always came out as "dok".) We made some headway this way, but I wanted to be a little more scientific about it, so I lent her a recorder and gave her a page of words. That was a Friday; I told her to make up a good recording during the weekend going over the list in a couple different ways.

On the Monday following this I did not go to school. A friend from out of town was visiting. Besides that, I wanted to test the waters on skipping class. And besides that, I was having serious misgivings about such a waste of time and whether or not to continue with the program. When I did show up on the Tuesday, Felicia returned my recorder and said she had been afraid she wouldn't get the chance to give it back. I could see the relief in her eyes. And I could see too that we were already more than friends. I felt bad then to have been contemplating abandoning her to our classmates. They were good people, but none was a kindred spirit — and that means everything in the world.

For reasons already discussed, there was absolutely nothing wrong here with Felicia's conduct. She was free to love. Moreover, reasoning along the same vein, she had no responsibility whatsoever toward Pyotr, her oppressor and tyrant, whether to enlighten him as to her disaffection or to treat him with the sort of fidelity required in any true marriage. Myself, now that is a different story. Had I known at this time Felicia's real situation, that would have been one thing, and I would have been on the same moral ground as she was on. However, I did not and thus was not. If I want to be a lawyer about it, I can point out that I was not the one party to any matrimonial contract, and therefore not responsible for its maintenance. But we all know that's just weasel talk. In our society the unwed partner in adultery may not have any direct responsibility toward the specific marriage contract that has been broken, yet is nevertheless an adulterer. I can plead some sort of subconscious cognizance of Felicia's state of abuse — and I have often told myself just such a thing; but this is belied by the fact that when she did reveal to me her real situation, I felt genuine shock along with my outrage. This leaves me with little else but to acknowledge the moral ambiguity of my position. In my own defense, though, I would like to emphasize that while I was ready for a little adventure, a little mischief, I was as concerned, I made myself as concerned, for Felicia's interests and well-being as if they were my own. I cared for her as for any other true friend. I never seduced her. Our friendship, our love, developed naturally, unaided by design.

Chapter 6

No, Reader, I had no desire to seduce Felicia. My notion of love
follows the lines laid down by romanticism, which I perceive to
be an outgrowth of Christianity. Paul describes love so perfectly:

If I speak in the tongues of men and of angels, but have not love,
I am only a resounding gong or a clanging cymbal. If I have the
gift of prophecy and can fathom all mysteries and all knowledge,
and if I have a faith that can move mountains, but have not love,
I am nothing. If I give all I possess to the poor and surrender my
body to the flames, but have not love, I gain nothing. Love is
patient, love is kind. It does not envy, it does not boast, it is not
proud. It is not rude, it is not self-seeking, it is not easily
angered, it keeps no record of wrongs. Love does not delight in
evil but rejoices with the truth. It always protects, always trusts,
always hopes, always perseveres. Love never fails.

To embody love thus is my ideal.

No, I neither desired nor sought to seduce Felicia. If love were to
grow naturally of its own accord between us, I wanted nothing
more nor less than to allow it to blossom forth as it would. The
fact that she was married was not the unequivocal barrier one

might think it should be. Obstacles to love, ironically enough, actually work to validate or certify true love because they demonstrate the overcoming of self-interest. I doubt if there are many people who are more puritanically suspicious of their own motives in love than am I. Obstacles to love are thus not only acceptable to me, they have always been downright necessary.

Our love was so innocent! Can you guess when we first kissed? Valentine's Day. We had known each other six weeks by then, spent five weeks together. The time spent together in those five weeks was as exclusively our own as if we'd been on so many dates. Consider it in that light: Twenty-five dates. How many couples have waited so long just for their first kiss? By their twenty-fifth date, many couples are already engaged, some even married. Our classmates assumed much, much earlier — it was obvious in their eyes — that we were doing much, much more. We didn't care. We just did our own thing.

On the Saturday before Valentine's, or the one a week earlier, Felicia came over to my place in the morning and cooked me a special breakfast of peroghies. A few days previously we'd had an important test and I had made a particularly extensive contribution toward her successful performance. This was her way of rewarding me. She made the peroghies from scratch right there as I watched. She also whipped up some crepes, which she called omelettes. I made a pretence of assisting her and mostly got in the way while she clucked and scolded me in Polish. Need I tell you, Reader, just how delicious the meal was? The peroghies were fried in butter, then served with sour cream. We put sour cream and blueberries on the "omelettes", which may sound a little strange but was delicious. She didn't have much time because she was ostensibly grocery shopping; but I had the stereo on, so after we had eaten we danced a little. Then she was off.

Soon after that came Valentine's Day, and for Valentine's I gave Felicia a story I had written. It sounds funny now as a gift — one might wonder whether such a thing could be a gift or merely an expression of vanity, but I meant it as representing a part of myself. I had gotten a nicely bound notebook and copied the whole thing, twenty or thirty pages, by hand. The story itself was, I believe, interesting and of decent quality. It was based on a dream I'd had long before. There was no special significance in it, as pertaining to us. In fact, if anything, it was quite post-romantic. I left it for her in the locker we shared and told her there was a surprise there waiting for her. As for myself, I had to go to a dentist appointment that day and was leaving class early, so Felicia got to spend the afternoon alone with our classmates.

I returned home from that dentist trip in the late afternoon feeling kind of lousy. My mouth was sore and stale-tasting. My lips felt like they had been stretched way out of shape, which they had been. You would be hard-pressed anytime, Reader, to describe me as a Lothario, and more than ever the way I looked and felt that day. When the doorbell rang, it didn't even occur to me that it would be Felicia. There wasn't time, what with her having to take the LRT all across town just to get to her car. All the same, it was her. This perked me up.

It's funny how we can spend so much time with people we love and yet still feel a thrill of delight on getting an unexpected few extra minutes with them just out of the blue like that. Felicia and I were as happy as children. We chatted a little. The time was already getting on and we could feel its shadow. We decided to dance. Then after a nice, slow dance, close and intimate, we kissed. I really have to smile to think of the state my mouth was in that day, of all days. Only a vampire could have savored kissing that beat-up maw.

Then Felicia was off and we two, separate in body yet joined in spirit, spent the rest of the evening in blissful yearning, right? Wrong. Then Felicia became regretful and teary, viewing herself as faithless and me as a wanton. This was so insulting to me. Believe me, Reader, I loved her. Had I not, I would've shown her out and slammed that door behind her forever. She started to cry and asked me why I was doing what I was doing. She looked at me as if I were a spider that had sat down beside her. I can't begin to describe to you the shock and indignation that was passing through my mind. Maybe I did not yet know that she was the victim of abuse, but it was plain as day that her marriage was a joke — if it even existed. Ever since we'd become acquainted I had suspected — and at times assumed — that she was already divorced, or at least separated. She never wore her wedding ring, and her comments on Pyotr had always been overwhelmingly negative, touching not only on his actions but frequently on his very character as well. And here she was with me, need I add? So now why, suddenly, was I supposed to be honoring this union for which she had made it amply clear she herself had no respect?

I knew Felicia was delicate. I knew she was conflicted. I loved her. Therefore, I held my peace. I told her I meant her no harm and that I thought that what we felt, and were doing, was mutual. I left it at that. I saw her to the door. This was something she was going to have to resolve in her own mind.

The day after Valentine's I slept in. I had a good, long sleep and got caught up on some much-needed rest. Do you think I was going to go to school, Reader? You bet I wasn't! By this time I was so thoroughly fed up with that program and the peanuts I got out of it for the full-time hours it cost me that the only thing keeping me in attendance was my friendship with Felicia.

Around nine or so my phone rang. I knew it was Felicia. I

ignored it. I really didn't want to talk to her just yet. It rang a few more times before I left the house.

I had nothing I had to do that day. It was a windfall, free to be splurged. I'd been meaning for some time to get a new pair of dress shoes, so I put on my nice charcoal suit and set out to find some. When I returned home later in the afternoon, the phone rang again. I was willing now to answer it. My feeling toward Felicia was not one of anger. Nor was I trying to punish her, to get even for what was all but a slap in the face the previous evening. To me, an overwhelmingly important element of love is equality, mutuality. My relationship with Felicia would have meant nothing to me if I'd thought it was merely a device of my own making. She had taken a step back. If she wanted to go on, it had to be unequivocally clear to me that it was her decision under no pressure from me. I wasn't looking for any self-abasement on her part, or even for an apology. She just had to return to the fold on her own two legs.

When I answered the phone, I could hear the worry in Felicia's voice. Was I sick? No, I just didn't feel like going to school today. She missed her kochania. Her voice was tender, sad. Her kochania missed her too. Was I going to school tomorrow? Yes, I was. She brightened. What had I been doing today? She had tried to call me all day. I told her. We talked for a while. We were back on track. It was months later when she asked if I would have returned to school had she not phoned me that day. Not that she needed to ask.

GARY WILSON

Chapter 7

Fragile. Felicia was so delicate and fragile. She was like a China doll. A sorrowful little China doll.

Have you ever been stuck outside in a howling blizzard, Reader? With the freezing wind passing through your clothing like it was gossamer and tearing at your hands and cheeks with a grip beyond pain? With stinging particles of ice being flung like darts at you from all directions? All you wanted to do was get inside away from the agony. And do you remember how you sat there once you had escaped the elements? The storm was outside and you were in. You had changed your frozen clothes for a thick, fluffy bathrobe and a mug of hot chocolate, and you were baking in front of a roaring fire, parked way too close. Yet, sitting there where all was well and Old Man Winter no longer threatened anyone, you kept catching yourself still getting all tensed up, fists and teeth clenched, even giving a little shudder now and then.

Every Monday when Felicia came to school, her teeth were clenched and she was a bundle of nerves. I noticed this right from the beginning, though at first I didn't understand the cause. It was incredibly disturbing. She was this way throughout the entire morning, invariably, and while she usually began to relax through the afternoon, occasionally her condition lasted into Tuesday. The cause was Pyotr, of course. Seldom has there been such a domineering person as him, a person for whom nothing can ever be right. Throughout the week his work engaged and preoccupied him enough that his brutality was suppressed; not so the weekends. Poor Felicia! Pyotr spent his weekends micromanaging her every move, driving the dear girl halfway up the wall with his constant demands. And when he found her lacking in any little way, which he inevitably did, over and over and over, he screamed and yelled at her, berating her the way a slave driver might a slave. Coming to school each week was Felicia's rest and relaxation, her chance to recuperate and recover her strength for the next weekend with Pyotr. I often felt toward her exactly as a doctor must feel toward his patients, just wanting to nurse and nurture her back to health.

Felicia was fragile in another way. She was pregnant. She suspected it in late January and confirmed it in February. We were on the LRT home one day when she asked me, I thought, if I'd still be her friend if she was a redhead. I figured she was thinking of dying her hair. I preferred her blonde, but it was none of my business, nor was it any big deal. What had struck me was the plaintive way she had asked the question, as if my opinion on her hair color mattered. I told her reassuringly that I would always be her friend no matter what color her hair was. This left her as puzzled as I had just been and after we got our crossed wires uncrossed we both had a good laugh.

Felicia's pregnancy summoned up something primordial within me, Reader. I am convinced that there is some sort of pheromone released by pregnant women that heightens men's innate protective instincts. Generally, I like to think of myself as the kind of guy who is willing to sacrifice himself to a reasonable degree for the protection of the weak. I hope this is true. But while Felicia was pregnant, specifically while she was in a state of pregnancy, and increasingly as it advanced, I felt a most powerful, even ferocious, urge to shield her from all sources of harm.

The underlying fragility of all, though, with Felicia was her overwhelming melancholy. It pervaded every aspect of her being. I have no doubt that if she was not born with it she had come to possess it fully in early childhood. It was too completely manifested in her to be any later overlay. Though I'm fairly convinced now that something so deep within the soul is essentially unalterable, at the time I was under the impression that it was caused solely by the toxic home atmosphere and so I tried to do what I could to help her overcome it. Such melancholy was simply foreign to me. I found it baffling. My outlook on life could not comprehend heartfelt pessimism, except perhaps on behalf of the unintelligent, which Felicia is not.

What did I do to try to help Felicia come out of her depression? Confronted with this question, all I can do is roll my eyes and let out a sigh in exasperation. What didn't I do? I did not pamper her — at least, not that until her pregnancy was well progressed and justified special treatment; but I did do my very best to treat her right at all times, to treat her the way I've always seen my father treating my mother. I wanted her to understand, not only on the intellectual level, that brutality is not the norm in relationships, neither physical nor psychological brutality. I wanted her to experience normality. Maybe then she would believe it existed.

Was I trying to come between Felicia and her husband, Reader? No. I was already there. Even as early as sometime in January, Felicia's emotional dependence was directed primarily towards me, if I'm not mistaken. Later, as I began to realize this, I did not discourage it at all, and in fact I encouraged it. I wanted to strengthen Felicia emotionally. If Pyotr was going to beat her down every time she stuck her head up to gasp for air, all the help in the world would be no use to her. I did not, could not, trust him with her emotional wellbeing. Therefore, after it was clear that she had transferred such dependence to me, I didn't surrender it back to him at any time.

What about the future? I consciously avoided making long-term plans or projections for my relationship with Felicia. The main reason for this stance was my perception of love and the necessity of its natural, unforced development. But besides that, there were the various imperatives that confused matters greatly.

It was obvious that Felicia's relationship with Pyotr was unsalvageable; yet did this mean that she ought to terminate the marriage? Pyotr was a good provider. There is no doubting that. He provided economic security for both Felicia and her offspring. This is undeniably significant. And even if she did choose to end her marriage, would she be able to? Would it be safe for her to do so? What would the effect be on her young son? My own attitude was that no amount of economic security in the world was worth the personal violation of the physical abuse, and even moreso the danger, the potentially life-threatening danger, it represented. Felicia knew my thinking on this, but I never harped on it, I never tried to pressure her into making a decision. It was not my place to do so. The union between her and Pyotr was hers to maintain or sunder, not mine. She was the one at the center of the swirl of factors who had to live with the outcome of her decision, not me. My course was to play the supporting role in whatever she decided to do. If she was to stay with Pyotr, I wanted to strengthen her both emotionally and informationally so that she could hopefully put an end to the abuse. If she was to leave him, she knew she could count on me to do all I could to help her make her way on her own. Would this latter be the prelude to marriage between her and myself? Looking even that far down the road was off-limits to me, no matter that it was an obvious extrapolation. I would've felt compromised in my concern for Felicia's interests if I myself were to become inextricably insinuated into the middle of it all in that way.

I have been talking about my relationship with Felicia and focusing almost exclusively on her and myself. In one sense this is an accurate focus, extremely so. However, there was a much larger aspect involved as well. My love for Felicia was a dialogue between me and God. It was my offering to heaven as the best I could give of what was most important. I felt that if two people were to love each other perfectly, to love each other with a perfect love, it might just make a difference to the whole world, the whole of human experience; it might just have some great metaphysical significance. I know how starry-eyed that sounds. I blush to make the disclosure. I just want you to understand how driven I was to treat Felicia perfectly, to love her perfectly, quite beyond all other considerations, good, bad and indifferent. I want to be able to tell you how very gentle I was with her without you taking it as me vaunting myself. This was something completely outside of myself; not strength or goodness of character, but rather the attempted transcendence of my admitted weakness and failings of character.

That said, I would be giving you a false impression if I left you with the idea that I was being something of an enormous down comforter for Felicia, insulating her from all the sharp edges of life, including those originating with me. Our love had all the playfulness and kidding around as any other. When I use the word "gentleness", I guess I mean always interacting in a positive way. If criticizing, then criticizing constructively, never destructively. Refraining from dominating, or any such urge. Fostering the full, independent development of the other person.

There was one time, however, and to my knowledge it was the only one of any significance, when I stumbled in my treatment of Felicia. As I have told you, Reader, she always made a lot of lunch and shared it with me. Well, at some point she somehow got it into her head that I was too restricted in my culinary experience and needed to be exposed to some of the more exotic foods in existence. Accordingly, she started bringing some of the most outlandish and disgusting crud imaginable to school and feeding it to me. I could hardly refuse this stuff without seeming impolite, but sometimes it was all I could do to get it down without puking my guts out. I am talking blood sausage, head cheese and worse things unnamable. Keep in mind that Felicia is east European. This went on for a while and I was to the point where I almost dreaded seeing her pull out lunch. I tried to give her the hint that this particular little ha-ha was no longer fun for the both of us, but she was not getting it. I finally ended up way overreacting. It is not like I yelled or even exhibited anger, but my comments cut far too close to the bone. To Felicia, her cooking was an expression of herself. Moreover, this was something she could give me, could do for me; it was an element of significance in her contribution toward the equilibrium of our relationship.

It's perverse, but true, that whereas insults at the hands of disagreeable people are easily tolerated by most of us, those coming from normally agreeable people are so painful as to be all but unacceptable. It's all a matter of conditioning.

Felicia took my rejection of her food as the rejection of herself. She was really upset. This was in the early afternoon that day after the lunch break. She was near to tears, hurt and angry. She refused to speak to me. We sat beside each other in silence until the coffee break. Then she wanted to go to our locker to clear her stuff out. We left the classroom before I tried to reason with her. I was not going to give the busybodies among our classmates the opportunity to gloat at the discord between us.

At that time we had a locker in a far building because everything near was taken. I am a man and a Canadian — or more pertinently, a Calgarian — and so you know I hate to admit it, Reader, but Felicia and I were both misty-eyed by the time we got to this locker. All she could say, over and over, was that now she knew I was like everyone else. There was no reasoning with her. I tried to apologize, but that was no use. Had our love not been real, this would have been the end of the relationship.

Felicia was insulted. She was hurt, cut to the quick. Maybe at that moment she was indeed disillusioned with me, as she said. More toward the truth, I believe, is simply that she was conflicted and the conflict within her seized upon the situation as a context for manifesting itself. I have made only brief mention of her conflict, but it was nothing to sniff at. She often worried that God would punish her or her unborn baby for our relationship. There was always a part of her that just wanted her home to be the happy, ideal home we all dream of; and this urge was so strong that it, for its part, idealized Pyotr's abusiveness away either to nothing or to a somewhat justified response to her own failings. It was this inner conflict of Felicia's, or more precisely the Mr. Hyde part of it, more than anything else, which was assailing our relationship that afternoon.

I opened the locker. I didn't want to. I asked Felicia not to remove her stuff, at least to think it over more first. She asked me why. Her movements began to be slow, but she was still beginning to sort things around out of the locker. I knew why. I loved her and she loved me. That was why. Simple.

Do you know, Reader, this was sometime in April, yet Felicia had never told me she loved me. We had been close, and ever closer, for three months plus. I had told her the same a million times, every time she asked and then some. Yet she had never said it to me. I never asked her to, mind you. I knew she loved me. Some things I trust more the less words get involved.

When Felicia asked me why she shouldn't clear her stuff out of the locker, she was kneeling on the floor facing the locker. I thought about her question for a moment, then I squatted down to be on her eye level. I looked deeply into her eyes. She could see the earnestness in my gaze. I don't know if I've ever been more earnest in my life.

"Because you love me," I said.

Felicia's fever broke. And so did the wellsprings of her eyes. Both of us were aghast at how close we'd just come to parting ways. Mr. Hyde had done his dirtiest, but he was left to limp off the field in failure.

Chapter 8

Felicia and I had all kinds of adventures, some due merely to our free-spiritedness, but most revolving around the fact that she was married. When I say "adventures", you know I just mean little frights and crises. One of these came the day she introduced me to Pyotr.

Reader, you would think that two people spending forty-five waking hours together a week would be more than sated with each other, no matter how in love they might be. We were not. We could have been spending one hundred and sixty-eight hours together, waking, and still not have been satisfied. We could have been spending one hundred and sixty-eight times one hundred and sixty-eight waking hours together and still be left begging for more. That's just how we were. That's just how love is. If you have ever really been in love, you know this. There were too many worlds and universes left to be explored behind each other's eyes for us to be content with that which was already in our hands.

It must have been late April when Felicia decided to introduce me to Pyotr. This was no decision to be taken lightly. I don't need to describe to you the potential perils it entailed. For my own part, though I did not anticipate in the least enjoying Pyotr's company and I knew that without a doubt I would be in a constant state of stress, these were minor considerations in contrast to getting a few precious extra hours now and then with my beloved. I was already well aware of Pyotr's abusive character. Felicia had finally told me all about this a month or more earlier.

It was my suggestion that Pyotr meet Felicia and me at school after class let out on the chosen day, well after class let out. You don't need me to tell you that neither Felicia nor I wanted him meeting any of our classmates. He worked in an office tower downtown, so it was a simple thing for him to hop on the LRT and take it the few stops to where we were. We would all then go to the gym and play racquetball for a while before getting into my car and finding a restaurant to eat at.

I was understandably nervous as I waited with Felicia at the LRT station. There were so many things that could go wrong. What if a lingering classmate walked by and made some friendly yet disastrous remark, not realizing who Pyotr was? Or what if Felicia or I let something slip out as we talked that might give him even an inkling as to how things really stood between us? Or what if we even just let it show in our eyes? I felt like wearing a balaclava and shades, just to be on the safe side. The thought of absent-mindedly brushing my fingertips down Felicia's spine in the small of her back gave me the willies and made me want to keep my hands stuffed deep into my pockets the whole time. Pyotr arrived and Felicia introduced us. Smiles all around. There was no ice to be broken. Pyotr was personable and we got off to a fine start. He was about my size, average height, average weight. He was a little stocky, whereas I am fairly slender. We both had brown hair. His face was unmistakably Russian (his mother is Russian). We chatted a little, went over the usual pleasantries — but not at all in a shallow, unfriendly way, and then headed into the gym to play some racquetball.

Pyotr had never played racquetball before, but his coordination was good and he made a respectable showing for a beginner. Felicia and I had played a few times, so she had the basic gist of the game. We all three hit the ball around together on the court for a while as I went over with Pyotr how the game was played. Then we played. Two would have a game while the third would rotate out and rest. Everything went unremarkably. No impressive moves were seen and none of us exerted him- or herself enough to become fatigued, but we had fun. And nothing went wrong.

The trouble came when we went to my car.

A few weeks earlier Felicia had needed to do some pressing errand right after lunch and she'd taken my car. It may have been a doctor's appointment she was going to. I would have driven her myself, but by this time the program coordinator was already getting so uptight about attendance that it would have drawn too much heat for both of us to disappear like that. So I stayed in class and Felicia took care of that business on her own. She was grateful for the use of my car, and when she drove back in to the parking lot she thought of a cute way to express her thanks. She would use her lipstick and draw a little heart on the windshield of my car. And that is exactly what she did. She whipped out her favorite shade of red lipstick and, on the inside top corner of the passenger's side, she drew a heart. It was maybe two inches across, discreet yet distinct. When I saw it, it warmed my heart. Every time I saw it, it warmed my heart.

Now, Reader, you know I had never wiped that heart of Felicia's off my windshield. And you know it was still just lurking there, waiting to touch off some incalculable devastation of one form or another. I was so used to its being there by this time that the thought of it never occurred to me until we had left the gym and were approaching my car. To Pyotr's knowledge, Felicia had never even been in my car before, much less riding in it with me daily and having used it on her own on occasion. Seeing her lipstick on my windshield — and as Felicia later confirmed to me, there was no chance that he would not have recognized the distinctive shade as her favorite — and in the shape of a heart, no less, would have been a disaster of the utmost magnitude.

I thought fast. Could I give the sunshade a nonchalant flip down to conceal the heart? That was more than iffy. It was evening by this time and the sun would not be in anybody's eyes by any stretch of the imagination. Such a move would only look unnatural and draw attention, if anything. Besides which, the swivel on that sunshade was super-stiff. Could I run ahead and wipe the heart off with my sleeve while Pyotr looked on and wondered what kind of weirdo he was about to get a ride from? That might be ever-so-slightly better than nothing at all, but ultimately it could not but leave Pyotr suspicious, all too suspicious. How I wished I had thought of Felicia's heart even a few minutes earlier! I could have left the two of them at the gym door and retrieved the car like I was some kind of good host.

Just as we were reaching my car a brainstorm struck me. The car was parked nose-in in its stall, and we were approaching along the lane so that we came at it from behind. I opened the trunk and told Pyotr and Felicia to toss their things in there. As they did so, I quickly slipped up the passenger's side and got the door opened, for them of course, me being the good host. Do I need to tell you that in about two milliseconds I had snatched the T-shirt out of my gym bag, wiped the windshield spotless — heartless, that is, and heaved the bag, T-shirt, heart and all, into the backseat of my car? I walked back to Pyotr and Felicia without missing a beat just as Pyotr was closing the trunk. Felicia caught my eye. She looked like she had just seen a ghost. I knew exactly

67

what was going through her mind, but there was no way for me to reassure her that all had been taken care of. I told them they would have to fight over the front seat, and I got in the driver's side.

Felicia ended up getting in the backseat. You have seen a child watching a scary movie, Reader, holding her hands over her face and peeking out between her fingers? That's about how Felicia looked as she climbed in, not daring even to glance towards where she knew the heart was. The fact that the sunshade was up, not down, only increased her trepidation. She had been hoping beyond hope that it had been left down, or that I had somehow put it down when I opened the door. But amazingly to her, there was no explosion the instant Pyotr got in, nor in the instants following that one. After a good long moment, she finally summoned up the courage to steal a peak at the dreaded spot. You should have seen the look of bewildered relief on her face (which I enjoyed with an innocent smile of my own for her), the confusion of questions in her eyes. She knew the heart was there, she knew it! She had been in my car at lunchtime when we had gone to the mall; she would have missed it had it been gone. Then we'd been together all afternoon; there was no chance in the world I'd slipped out to my car even for a minute. She had watched me open the trunk and the passenger door for her and Pyotr. She had even delayed Pyotr a little at the trunk on purpose to give me the chance to force the sunshade down, only to witness, with disgust and agitation, my immediate return. There was no way that I could have done anything of any use in that time, no way at all. That the heart was gone and in its place was nothing but clear sky was little short of a miracle, a most welcome miracle, to be sure, but a miracle no less, a reprieve sent from heaven above.

I, cruel heart, had to leave poor Felicia in her perplexed state. How could I say anything with Pyotr there? All I could afford was a bit of a Mona Lisa now and then. It was the next morning before I could at last relieve her of all her pent-up suspense. What a good laugh we had then! Living and reliving each and every moment and fear from our two different perspectives. We really did have a very, very close call.

GARY WILSON

Chapter 9

Felicia was pregnant. Let me tell you now, Reader, about her pregnancy, her high-risk pregnancy.

Felicia was Rh-positive. Her blood type was A-positive, whereas Pyotr's blood type was O-negative. I may have the positives and negatives mixed up here, and I may be a little imprecise in my knowledge of all this, but I will explain it the best I can.

It is only or primarily women that are Rh-positive. Men are usually or always Rh-negative. But even among women, it is a small minority that are Rh-positive. This small minority experience problems in pregnancy when the babies they carry are Rh-negative. The two kinds of blood cannot mix. If they do, a toxic reaction sets in and can result in the loss of the mother's life. Birth is the most critical time of all because so much potential exists for such an admixture. However, all throughout pregnancy a woman in such a situation must be very careful and undergo frequent tests to ensure that the child's development is progressing without problem. A miscarriage, and particularly an unforeseen and sudden miscarriage, holds every bit as much danger for the mother as a difficult birth. This is why such a pregnancy is called a high-risk pregnancy.

When our classmates eventually learned that Felicia was expecting, a lot of them assumed that I was the father. This was natural enough. After all, Felicia and I conducted ourselves like nothing other than a couple newlyweds. We treated that program like one long honeymoon. We both would have loved for me to have been the child's father — I can't tell you how many million times we talked about that — but it was impossible that it was so. Felicia's baby was conceived in mid-January. Yet I can tell you this, Reader, that although I did not father the child, I did what I could to contribute to his wellbeing. His mother and I were together, intensively together, all throughout his gestation; we could hardly have been more together had we been Siamese twins. My voice was constantly in Felicia's ears, and thus the child's as well. Every waking moment of her serenity during that pregnancy was found in my presence, often enough in my arms and caresses. Both Felicia and I were aware that the human environment of the unborn has a tremendous influence on later development and character. Together we did everything we could to provide her baby with the very best, the very happiest, of pre-birth existences.

Some will say that Felicia and I could have been doing no good whatsoever for her child by our intimacy. If you view our relationship as immoral with no possible justification, then it's logical to go from there that no good could come out of it. I disagree with this assessment, but it is the consistent expression of a perspective that I respect tremendously, a perspective on life held by people I respect tremendously. On the other hand, if you accept that there was an integral innocence in Felicia's actions from the very start, and my own from the time I became aware of her abused state, then you can see how we sincerely felt that the way we were conducting ourselves, our intimacy, far from being detrimental to the child's unseen growth, was the very best thing we could be doing for him. We were giving him the window on a normal, loving relationship that he would not be getting otherwise.

Felicia and I had our share of passion. Far more than our share, actually. Yet you can see without me telling you that the romance between us was not pursued with an eye to the ecstasy, but oriented instead around the intimacy. Our relationship may have moved in the physical realm, but it was equally spiritual in nature. It should not surprise you then, Reader, that even as we allowed ourselves no end of play in the early months of her pregnancy, once Felicia began to feel and show the effects of her condition, we set aside all the more physical, sensual, part of our intimacy without the slightest hesitation.

It was in May that Felicia and I had our last bit of frolicking while she was still pregnant. Her tummy was just barely beginning to show the tiniest of bulges. It was such a beautiful spring day, the sort of day you can find only in the foothills with

the fresh, pine-laden air and the gentle fingers of the sun
reaching down through the tree branches.

For some reason, class had let out an hour or so early that day.
This was an unusual and most welcome event. Felicia and I were
like a couple of kids with a pocketful of candy. What were we
going to do with ourselves? Since the weather was so nice and
we had enough time for something beyond the regular routine of
going to a mall or stopping for a few snatched moments at my
place, we jumped into my car and drove out to the mountains
past Bragg Creek. This is only maybe twenty miles from the city
limits, but civilization is entirely left behind. We found a
secluded place and there had the great outdoors all to ourselves.
What a luxury! Parks in the city always seemed to have no end
of pedestrians, peeping about, sneaking here and there, always
popping up when they're least wanted. There was a fire pit
where we stopped, and above this rose a wooded incline. It was a
little ways up this slope, in the shade of the trees under the blue
sky, that we spent the rest of that afternoon. I can still smell the
pine and moss mingled together.

From this time onward, until after Felicia had had her baby, we
engaged in no greater physical intimacy than the occasional kiss.
And even that, after about the middle of June, we limited to what
was perfectly fraternal. We were taking no chances with
Felicia's health and her baby's well-being.

Chapter 10

I wish I could express to you the depth and breadth of the intimacy between Felicia and myself, Reader. It was of a nature that surely seldom appears.

Imagine if all the waters of the Pacific were piled up in a single mighty wave that swept across the entire Eurasian landmass from China to the tip of Iberia. Every leaf, twig and branch of every tree and shrub would be touched. Every one of a million hamlets, towns and cities would be inundated. Every bit of rock and soil, from the flats of Holland and Bangladesh to the heights of Everest and Elbrus, would be drenched. Nothing in all the land would be untouched by such a wave. This is how it was with Felicia and me. We swept through each other, tirelessly embracing any and every one of the million, trillion, aspects of each other we encountered.

It was the similarity, the exactitude of the similarity, of the deepest essence of our beings that allowed Felicia and me such intimacy. There was a peculiar resonation between us that, in spite of all the superficial differences, drew us inexorably closer and closer. We came to view each other as something akin to spiritual twins, like as if some soul before time had been split in two and incarnated in both of us.

Children have the sort of intimacy Felicia and I had. That's because they have not yet learned to wear masks, layer upon layer upon layer of masks. Is it our dysfunctional society-in-turmoil that causes this weaving and wearing of masks as children mature into youth and adulthood, or does such a thing happen in all societies no matter how established and serene? Some of my favorite books in childhood addressed this very subject in allegory, the betrayal of childhood, of selfhood. The animals in the Chronicles of Narnia that were fully alive, that fully experienced life, were the talking animals; whereas the dumb animals lived on a lower plane of existence, mere subsistence. These dumb animals were animals who had — or whose ancestors had — betrayed their very souls, subverted their wills, bowed the knee to Mammon, sold out the freedom, the individuality, of their childhood to the sirenic chains, the domestication, of adulthood. The talking animals looked at them, quite rightfully, with nothing but pity and contempt. John Christopher in 'The White Mountains' illustrated the same concept by depicting an alien-controlled society where the rite of passage into adulthood involved the surgical implanting of a device that governed the will. Even in the tales of that scapegrace, the Great Brain, we find echoes of betrayal – the betrayal of both shared ideals and self-respect – as the older boys discover girls in a whole new way and leave the younger boys to their own devices. You can begin to see the intense revulsion I have always felt, from an early age onward, toward the betrayal of my own individuality, the subversion of self to society. None of this is to say that I do not wear masks, that both Felicia and I did not have our full complement of masks. But we, as talking animals, knew that between the two of us there was no need for them, no need for any of them.

I wrote a poem a few years before I met Felicia that fit her perfectly, so perfectly as to have been prophetic, if you believe in the possibility of that kind of thing. The name of this poem was 'Zuhdoethekaunee'. I created this name of my unknown and untamable true love, my ideal love, because I liked the sound of its flow. (The primary accent is on the second syllable.) I gave a copy, my only copy actually, of this poem to Felicia for her birthday. I also bought her a pretty little compact and had it engraved with the words "Where, O where, Zuhdoethekaunee", part of a line from the poem. A funny thing about that engraving was that I had opened the compact in the way natural for me to open and peer into it, and I'd shown the fool jeweler just exactly where I wanted the words to be, going over the spelling carefully so as not to have a tragedy. Then, instead of piping up and telling me I had the thing sideways, he just stupidly nodded and marked down my instructions precisely. He even had a female assistant there who should have noticed what was going on and pointed out that my words were climbing where they should have been reclining. When I gave it to Felicia, she couldn't help but giggle at my mistake. I would've taken it back to replace the mirror and have it engraved again properly, but she said No, she loved it just the way it was, that such an error could only be done by a book-lover. Whenever she would use it, it would remind her that much more of me. So I left it as it turned out and we both had a good chuckle.

I wish I could remember the words of 'Zuhdoethekaunee'. I would record them for you right here if I could, Reader. They were, in my humble opinion, quite beautiful. They expressed, accurately and presciently, the completeness and naturalness of the intimacy between Felicia and me. However, I will share with you one line, the only complete line I remember. Even by itself it should give you an idea of the sentiment of the poem as a whole:

Eyes, but not lips, speaking to me;
alone we two within our throng.

School was not the only place that Felicia and I were alone among others. You should have seen us interacting together when I would visit at her house. I have to say that she was absolutely exquisite. I would liken this to a dance — in fact, always in my mind at the time I did look at it as simply that, a dance, a minuet for Pyotr to see. Never once did the eyes of either of us seek out those of the other for a cue. Never did our eyes rest on each other in blissful caress, not even for a split second. Never did Pyotr see in me anything beyond brotherly fondness for Felicia, or the same sisterly in her for me. Yet right there under his alert if not exactly vigilant gaze, we were gorging on each other's presence, drinking in each other's eventide proximity. Felicia needed not speak to me a single word in a quarter hour, yet I knew every thought, every wish, that passed through her mind in that whole time. I knew every beat of her heart, and she mine. We had no need of words, not even of glances. We could feel all as if our brains were somehow networked through the ether.

As spring progressed into summer, I was spending more and more extracurricular time at Felicia's, a minimum of one weeknight per week and always either the Saturday or the Sunday of each weekend. Ostensibly, I was Pyotr's friend. I was visiting the two of them, but visiting Pyotr more than Felicia because she had all kinds of household work to keep her busy. I did get along well with Pyotr, it is true, but there was no getting around the fact that he was a wife-beater. This disqualified him entirely from any possibility of being my genuine friend, or should I say, me from being his genuine friend. Had I just been Felicia's secret love, and her husband been a good guy, though it's unlikely real friendship would have arisen between us, it would nevertheless not have been an outright impossibility. As it was with Pyotr, there was never the slightest chance of friendship between us. This was as true in the summertime, after we had come to know each other well, as it was the day in March that Felicia had revealed to me his abuse. Contempt was the friendliest emotion I could feel for a man who beat his wife, for any man who would stoop to picking on the weak and helpless; and utter detestation was closer to how I actually felt. Yet I showed this no more than I showed my love for Felicia.

On a typical such visit, my arrival would come an hour or so before supper. I might play with Felicia's son a little, or go for a walk with him, or help him practice reading. He was only five or six years old. If Pyotr was already home from work, I would spend the time with him instead. I don't think either Pyotr or I ever helped with the cooking, but it seems like we may have set the table sometimes. The one exception to our abstinence from cooking was when there was barbecuing to be done, at which Pyotr was very adept. Then we would go out onto the backyard deck just outside the kitchen door and fire up the barbie.

Suppers were excellent at Felicia's whether the food came out of the oven or off the barbecue grill. There was always a good variety of offerings to choose from, maybe eight or ten dishes in total on average. For the life of me, I cannot remember what most of these dishes were, and more often than not they were Polish with no name in English anyhow. It's a good thing the food was good, because Felicia was always so anxious about my slender physique that she was making sure I had seconds and thirds of everything. For my part, the food was so good that I really could not have turned it down even if I had not had the further motivation of Felicia's love and concern. We would always linger over supper for a good hour or more, what with enjoying the food to the extent it deserved plus simply engaging in conversation. Poles take their hospitality very seriously. It is as important for them that everyone has a good, thorough visit while they eat as it is that all get filled bursting at the seams by the time dessert is done. And Polish desserts! If you are familiar with Polish cuisine, Reader, you know how their desserts are a world unto themselves. Who would ever think that ingredients like noodles and sour cream could ever show up to good advantage in dessert dishes? Yet they do, they most definitely do. Really, I don't want to think further about these suppers. It is little more than punishment to my now-deprived palate.

After supper, Pyotr and I would continue to visit while Felicia busied herself cleaning up. As often as not, he and I would practice his English pronunciation. This wasn't something that I was particularly keen on doing with him. It's one thing to sit in front of a pretty girl and watch her mouth carefully as she talks, or have her watch your own just as carefully so that she can imitate the posture and movements. Doing the same with a fellow male is quite another. Then you notice all the little peculiarities of human facial anatomy in a less than charming light. My love for Felicia was the only thing that could induce me to do this. For his part, Pyotr was highly motivated because he knew his accent was less than musical and he did not want any kind of disadvantage like this for his career.

Eventually the time would be getting on and the evening would wind down. I have said that Felicia and I were perfect in our dance of chastity before Pyotr's eyes. This does not mean that the odd opportunity didn't present itself every now and then for some little exhibition of affection. Pyotr might go to the washroom. He might go upstairs to change his clothes. One time after a particularly grueling day at the office, he fell asleep on the family room couch. We never took advantage of such opportunities in any perilous way. A longing look shared, a kiss blown across a room, a finger drawn across the nape of neck. That's all. Nothing left to reverberate. No cause for anxiety or lingering furtiveness.

Chapter 11

I've told you about Felicia's deep-seated melancholy, Reader.
Let me tell you now how hard I tried to help her overcome it.

Back in the winter months I didn't take this melancholy
seriously. It was incomprehensible to me. I may have shared
Felicia's substratum agnosticism; however, to me this led not to
apathy and disorientation, but rather to faith and to theorizing
and the scientific method, even to adventure, the adventure of
exploration and discovery. I could allow that hopelessness was
appropriate on the part of the lumpen proletariat, those masses of
human lemmings marked as such by their failure to fight against
the current. But we were the talking animals, the cities of light,
the very apex of the thing called life. No amount, no intensity, of
darkness could ever extinguish such as we, nor should
fundamentally dismay us in any way.

I might as well have been reasoning with the wind. One day
Felicia's sadness would seem to be overcome and I would let out
a sigh of satisfied relief. The next day it would be back with a
vengeance. I was like a little boy on the beach who thinks he is
chasing the water away down the sand, only to be caught full on
by the next wave as it crashes into shore. The Jesuits say, or used

to say, that if they were given a young mind to mold till the age of seven, it would be theirs for life. Well, looking back now, all I can say is that I'm afraid some Jesuit of Sorrow got a hold of young Felicia and never after let her out of his grasp.

I guess you could characterize my efforts for the first while as trying to cheer Felicia up; but by the time spring was rolling around, I had realized that she was needing more than a pick-me-up. Having become aware of the abuse, I focused on it as the cause of her melancholy. My purpose was to help her regain her faith in humanity, which was clearly so sorely lacking. I wanted her to taste genuine love. I wanted her to feel my love to the very core of her being. To that end I set out and wrote her a story.

Whenever I stop to think about it, as I am doing this very instant, I really become envious of good writers. They have such vast vocabularies, such variety of grammar, such depth of insight, such wit, such poetry. When my eye ranges over my own little ragtag of offerings, all unpublished to this day, and most, if not all, unpublishable as well, I see a flock of underfed sparrows, threadbare and dun beside the brilliant peacocks, birds-of-paradise and flamingoes Nabokov, Lawrence, Wilde, Hesse and others of their ilk have bequeathed us.

Speaking of sparrows, this story I wrote for Felicia was a fairytale involving a princess and a sparrow. I am afraid it was quite derivative, owing much to Sleeping Beauty and that little Happy Prince with his swallow friend who kept appearing, year after year, on CBC as the one animated special it was apparently able to afford, the annual bone it threw to that element of its underage target audience not gimp enough to partake of its regular fare. I'm sure we all remember the shades of blue and grey, the little bird who waited too long to head south, the heart and the hardened little lifeless form beside it that the workers found in breaking up the statue.

I hardly remember my sparrow story. I don't say it was good. But it was an expression of my love for Felicia. As such, it had a touching integrity to it, an earnestness I know she felt. Even as I sit here reminiscing, the vague image of it does come back to me. The princess was in a deep, magical sleep — or, as we moderns put it so poetically, a coma. The sparrow did everything he could to wake her; he searched the world wide for a cure, to no avail. Eventually nearing death, he senses his time has come and returns to her side, nestling by her with feelings of remorse for failing her. His last act is to give her a peck on the lips before expiring. Do I need to tell you what happened then, Reader?

Felicia was sweet in complimenting my fifteen- or twenty-page opus of love and, as I said, I do know it touched her. A few weeks later, I wrote her a second, but very different, story. I could not write another fairy tale, another typical fairy tale. The first one had integrity because I meant every word of it, no matter how well-worn and contrived the genre. Another similar would have been overkill. Instead, I came up with 'Vampyra', an anti-fairy tale. Its theme was unconditional love.

Again, as with the first story, my recollection of this one is very sketchy. I believe the setting is the Carpathian mountains, just north of Transylvania. There is a simple young woodsman. He has a betrothed. Theirs is a simple, uncomplicated love. The peace of the district is shattered by a vampire. Unapprehended, this vampire spreads terror throughout the region with its grotesque and monstrous predations. The good folk, the woodsman among them, rise up in arms to hunt down and destroy the menace. And yes, you guessed it: the vampire is none other than the woodsman's betrothed. What does he do when he alone learns of this? Does he wooden-stake her himself? Or does he lovingly banish her from the region? Or does he capture her and hand her over to the authorities? He does none of these things. He joins her, giving up hearth and home, friends and family, in fact everything, and the two of them flee to enjoy wandering lives together of blood-sucking and true love for all eternity.

'Vampyra' sounds awful, as I read back over these words. Twisted. Grotesque. Nevertheless, I stand one hundred per cent behind it, behind the theme it contains. The true artist subordinates everything else in his life to his art, does not care one bit for anything as compared to his art, sustains his very life solely for the purpose of pursuing his art. Similarly, true lovers love with abandon, reckless and complete. There is no bread. There is no home. There is no world. There is no time. There is no eternity. There is no rest. There is only one. Two, which are one.

The third and final story I wrote for Felicia was titled 'Neptunina'. You have got to know that it was about a mermaid. That pretty much covers all the bases of camp: a princess and a vampire followed by a mermaid. To this day, I do not know whether I was writing this last story more to Felicia or to myself. It was definitely the least well written of the three, yet at the same time it was certainly the deepest.

We all struggle, at one time or another in our lives, with the issue of identity. Who am I? Where did I come from? Why am I me, not him, not her? Am I eternal? How could this world, which I have no choice but to orient entirely around myself, exist if I did not? I know that I exist, really exist, but do all these others, who have in common that they are not me, really exist? This is not just some enormous, cosmic joke of perception, is it? And assuming all does exist, why? Why? Why!?

I first grappled with these questions at a very young age, maybe four or five. I don't know if that is precocious or normal. My thoughts and ideas were no more developed than you would expect, but I did take the whole subject quite seriously. I remember seeing ugly children and wondering how a loving God could be so cruel as to make them like that; my conclusion was that they didn't exist, that they were only drones or some such thing. I went from there to consider existence itself, others', my own, that of God. I suspect that many young children spend time thinking about things more profound than many would give them credit for, and more profound than the sorts of things that occupy the minds of the vast majority of adults. This may be one reason why a theme like the betrayal of childhood is so powerful.

I wrote 'Neptunina' in the middle of July. It was about this young mermaid who, as she grew into adulthood, became more and more suspicious and disillusioned with everything and everyone around her. She had the growing impression that she was alone, entirely alone, and that her world around her had animation only when she was perceiving it, freezing into rigidity otherwise. The sad part is that I cannot remember the denouement to this particular kettle of fish. Sadder still is that discontinuing the story at this point probably best represents the reality it was meant to combat.

I tried so hard to spark Felicia's faith in the possibility of good! I felt so bad for her trying to comprehend her complete and utter disillusionment with everything. I did all I could do to help her overcome it all. I sit here and shake my head in bewilderment trying to think of what else I could have done, or what else could be done. The problem lay at the very deepest level of her psyche. The abuse was certainly an aggravating factor, perhaps working to solidify previously amorphous attitudes of negativity, but the root of the problem was beneath and prior to even that.

Needless to say, my three stories, my effort to use allegory so as to help Felicia retool her philosophy and free herself from the debilitating quagmire of pessimism she was mired in, were of no appreciable effect. She may have gotten a little entertainment from them. I'm sure they warmed her heart. I doubt if they did anything beyond that. As for me, what I did beyond that was put my pen down and simply love my darling girl.

Chapter 12

Prior to August, I myself had never seen Pyotr's abusiveness. I had heard about it from Felicia, and I had seen its effects on her, but I'd never seen it with my own two eyes. What I had seen in Pyotr, though, was a pronounced misogyny. This misogyny's whole focus was male supremacy and the subservience of women, whether mother, wife or stranger. It had no threads of chivalry, protectiveness or responsibility to impart to it some sort of equilibrium. It was imperialism on the domestic scale, exploitation, pure and undiluted.

What confronted me one day in mid-August was not an actual physical assault, but rather verbal abuse. When I say "verbal abuse", Reader, you may get the impression of someone making unkind comments, maybe a supervisor dropping a pithy remark about some underling's mediocre performance or a coach goading his team into a better effort. It's true that unkind comments were involved here, but the verbal aspect was wholly secondary to the abuse aspect. This verbal abuse was simple, straightforward abuse frustrated in its flowering to the physical level only by the intrusion of company, the inconvenience of a witness being present. A pimp out on a street corner could not have excoriated his prostitute with any more vehemence, vileness, spite and foul language than I heard Pyotr using against Felicia that day, and I'm speaking for only what I heard in English — the Polish was probably twice as bad.

The thing that had touched Pyotr off was a dispute he was having with Felicia over the selling price of their home. He had been trying for some time to get a promotion and transfer within his company, the transfer being to Houston. Now that he had it, he was in a fret to get moved as soon as possible. He was wanting Felicia to sign some real estate papers authorizing the realtor to dump their house immediately at any selling price. He knew that his company would eat the difference between that price and their purchase price two or three years earlier, so he wasn't interested in taking the time to get top dollar. Felicia, on the other hand, felt their house was worth more than they had paid and she wanted to get fair market value out of it. She had, after all, put considerable effort into various improvements to it and was not inclined, as Pyotr was, to discount entirely their value.

Ever since he had gotten a new supervisor, a woman, a few months previously, Pyotr had been frantic to be moving on. There was nothing he could have found more unbearable than working under a woman. He often expressed his bitterness about the situation to me and I had to suppress many a smile thinking about the irony of it. Upon being notified of his acceptance to the Houston position, he moved at warp speed to try to effect the transfer immediately. If he'd had his way, and at first he tried hard to do so, it would have been complete within a week, Felicia entering her eighth month of a high-risk pregnancy and all. The only thing that actually stopped him was that no airline would allow Felicia aboard in her advanced state of pregnancy. The result was that Pyotr had to compromise and let her stay in Calgary until the baby was born while he would proceed to Houston and get settled into his new job.

Reader, through the spring and summer, I had become lulled to some degree in my perception of Pyotr. I knew what he was capable of. I was aware of his attitudes. I could see the psychological effects of it on Felicia. Yet it was only when I actually witnessed a live demonstration that I felt a real urgency about her immediate wellbeing. There is a profound difference between comprehending something intellectually and suddenly having to come to grips with it in the flesh. From that day of the verbal abuse in August onward, even though what I had witnessed had not become physical, my concern for Felicia jumped to the level of critical and stayed there permanently. And as it soon turned out, such heightened concern was not out of place in the least.

Pyotr made one trip to Houston and back in the latter part of August, then for most of the following month he would be returning there. But he was in Calgary for the Labor Day weekend.

The Saturday before Labor Day I had spent at Felicia's. Pyotr was a little keyed-up with all the excitement of impending change, but his manner was not particularly aggressive. The only thing remarkable that happened that evening was that a man came and bought their car. Pyotr arranged the sale so that he would keep the car a couple days more, till the Monday when he would be flying back to Houston. (Nothing illustrates Pyotr's misogyny better, actually, than his casual disposal thus of the family car. Felicia was six weeks now from giving birth. Their home was in an outlying area of the city, a fair distance from the nearest hospital. Felicia's only remaining form of transportation was the public transit system, meaning that she was about a fifteen-minute bus ride from the nearest LRT station, further yet from her doctor's office, the closest big mall and almost anywhere else she might want to go. Need I say more?)

I didn't talk to Felicia on the Sunday, nor on Labor Day. By then — that is, by that stage of our relationship, this was a little unusual, to go so long without contact, yet in itself it was no cause for concern. Felicia had a lot of things to get done. For my part, I never called her even now because I did not want to end up talking to Pyotr for hours. When she would call me, he would already be asleep or still be at work. That way we could chat nicely. Anyway, it was the Tuesday morning before I saw

Felicia.

I should mention that our schooling together was in its final phase at this point. Classes had finished in the latter part of August and we were now working on our practicum, a four-week project out in the real world. You already know without me telling you, Reader, that Felicia and I were assigned to the same project. (This was thanks mostly to our own efforts, but also to the fact that the poor old administrator did not dare to try and block us from working together.) We had to put in the time needed to complete the project successfully; but, within reasonable parameters, we were relatively free to manage our own time without a lot of supervision.

When I picked Felicia up that Tuesday morning at the bus-stop near her house, something was terribly wrong. She was trembling, a bundle of nerves. She wore a grimace of tension. She looked like somebody who had just been plucked out of icy waters and was at death's chilliest door. Whatever was wrong? What had happened?

On Sunday afternoon Felicia had been cleaning her house to get it spotless in case any prospective home-buyers came around. I think I already told you how spic-and-span she always kept the place. Nevertheless, she was getting it just a little spicker-and-spanner. She had barely finished manicuring the bathroom that

Pyotr always used when he decided he was going to shave. That was fine, of course. All she asked was that he wipe the sink area down when he finished so that it would look perfect again.

Well, Pyotr did not like this. Here he was, the breadwinner winning beaucoup bread — with a fresh promotion and transfer to boot, no less — and now his chattel was trying to get him doing women's work. Did she not understand the stress he was constantly under? Just because he hadn't set foot in the office in the last three days, that didn't mean he wasn't still feeling the effects of his workload. All he wanted was to shave in peace like a man, splash the cool water onto his face to soothe it, and then relax with the newspaper while his barefoot and pregnant dutifully played her own part. But there she was, slacking off and — worse yet — trying to slave drive him. Things were really beginning to get out of hand and it was all a guy could do to keep his cool. First he'd put up with her arguing a couple weeks earlier over the asking price for their home and now she thought she could just boss him around the house like he was her flunky. He was really starting to become angry. Correction. He was angry. Very angry.

Pyotr shaved. He splashed cool water onto his face. A lot of cool water. Then he was done, all done. He left the bathroom. And waited.

"Pyotr, I've been cleaning all day long. It wouldn't hurt you just to wipe up after yourself."

... Oh, chapka! You have just said the magic words...

Chapka, chapka, chapka! You still do not know who you're playing with — after all these years. I'm so patient with you. I ask so little of you. But now you leave me no choice. You're forcing me to respond in the only way left.

Pyotr yelled at Felicia and told her to wipe the sink down herself. She refused. She told him to. He exploded. He swore at her. He screamed at her. He hauled her into the bathroom and threw a towel in her face. She pushed it back at him starting to cry. She tried to get out past him. He grabbed her and smashed her against the wall. It was regrettable that she was seven and a half months into a high-risk pregnancy, but she had forced his hand, she had really been getting on his nerves and today she had gone too far. He was going to beat the living daylights out of her. It had been a long time coming. She needed it, even if she didn't realize it.

— Ding dong!

Two sets of ears cock up. One set hopeful, praying for relief. The other set hesitating, weighing factors.

Any other Sunday Pyotr would have ignored the door. A neighbor. A charity beggar. A Jehovah's Witness. A brat wanting a playmate. But today it could be a home-buyer. Decisions, decisions, decisions...

Decisions!

Pyotr cursed under his breath. He never deigned to give the cowering Felicia so much as a glance as he turned to go downstairs and answer the door.

It was a realtor. She wanted to go through the house from top to bottom and check it out thoroughly.

Felicia had gotten her reprieve. She went to bed with a splitting headache when the realtor left and stayed there all night and all day Monday until Pyotr left for the airport.

What would have happened if that doorbell had not rung, Reader? Pyotr would have beaten Felicia badly. Then she may have miscarried, possibly even have died. This was why she was still shaking when we met on the Tuesday morning. She felt that she had come within a hair of losing her baby, within a hair of losing her life.

Chapter 13

Allen Bill Pond. What does 'Allen Bill' mean? Is it someone's name? Is it the name of a species of bird? I assume the latter, but I don't actually know.

One time, a couple months earlier in July, Felicia and I had talked about marriage. We hadn't "talked about marriage" in the conventional meaning of that phrase; rather, we had discussed the topic in a way that was both far more and far less meaningful than that would entail. I can't remember what led into it — probably talk of love — but Felicia said to me, quite matter-of-factly, yet teasingly too, a sprite in her eye, "If I wanted you to, you would marry me."

This was a very simple and very complex question for me. The simple answer was, "Yes, of course," which I said without hesitation. We both already knew this was true, for there were no secrets between us, whether or not we'd gone over a matter. I enjoyed being with Felicia and I wanted us to remain together all throughout the future. As a vehicle, marriage is useful toward that end. Equally important, it seemed possible to me that Felicia would be incapable of leaving Pyotr, of exiting even such an abusive situation, without the security of knowing that an

alternative was available to her and immediately accessible.
Therefore, on two counts my simple answer to her was Yes.
Just as we both knew the simple answer, and its veracity, to the
simple question contained in Felicia's declaration, so also were
we both fully cognizant of the massive iceberg of complexity
lurking quietly beneath the simple waters. I was not, am not, the
marrying kind. I find the institution ridiculous; or, if not
ridiculous, then the destruction of the essence of what it's meant
to foster. The important thing, the underlying thing, the real
thing, is love. Marriage is to love what the bottle is to a genie,
what the Dead Sea is to the living Jordan. Containment.
Definition. Suppression. Suffocation.

Felicia knew as well as I did that if I were to marry her it would
be a marriageless marriage. No heartfelt professions of undying
love. No commitment to fidelity. No subversion of self. Nothing
other than an economic union, a business relationship designed
to secure for her the means to provide for herself and her
children all the necessities of life and normality. It had to be this
way. My love for her — our love for each other — necessitated
it. To tie our love to marriage would have been the death of it,
like pinning a butterfly onto a board for the world to see and
admire. To remain pure, to remain living and vibrant, our love
had to remain unbound, spontaneous. Every new day, every new
moment, was a new day, a new moment, a new discovery of
love. We had no responsibility to love. We loved because we

loved. We loved that we loved. We were two children, two innocents ancient of days, free to love and loving freely. What sort of fool is it who values more highly the bird in hand than the two, the trillion, in bush and sky? Marriage, society's convention of marriage, is the replacement of a relationship based on love, constantly renewed and renewing love, with one based on a contract, a shopkeeper's bond. (None of this is to say that people do not manage, in their different ways, to preserve love, true love, though caught in the teeth of wedlock. They do. Whether as serpents or as doves, they do — or at least some of them do.)

So Felicia and I talked that day in July about marriage. We verbalized what we already knew. We made no resolutions, never a commitment. We just discussed reality as it was. And this particular reality was the same at the time of Labor Day as it was in July.

When I saw Felicia on the Tuesday following Labor Day and learned of the peril she had been in, I was in a real quandary. Had I been right not to urge her to leave Pyotr? Certainly in theory such a course as mine had been was all well and good. It was a mark of respect. It was my sovereign will meeting her sovereign will on terms of perfect equality, neither submitting, neither dominating, just joining on the field that was common ground and ignoring the rest, fellow-traveling along that part of the path that we could share and accommodating the need to make solitary passage over the other parts. Who was I — or anyone, for that matter, who had never walked so much as a single step in Felicia's shoes to direct her on the course she should take in life? The very notion alone was enough to cause my sense of individualism, my exultation of the individual, to rise up within me in revolt.

In theory my stance was good, great, even divine. In reality it was deficient. It pains me to say this. The theory is so appealing. Moreover, I like to pretend to myself that I know everything, everything worth knowing. (Don't worry, Reader! I realize that I know nothing. In fact, I refine Socrates, who did claim one bit of knowledge, with, "I don't know that I know, but neither do I know that I don't know." This is true agnosticism, and the most useful.) Anyhow, I think by now you have been able to perceive that I am enough of a self worshipping know-it-all to derive genuine anguish from having to confront any glaring deficiency in my thought. Even today, as I think about and write this, I still see more chaos and confusion in the matter than satisfying resolution. It was right of me to be fastidious in my respect toward Felicia's exercise of her own will, studiously avoiding coercion in even the slightest degree. For heaven's sake, it was right! However, look at Labor Day: Had Felicia ended up dead, could I still maintain my rightness? Now, consider that it was chance, a toss-up, a door-bell ringing that could have come thirty seconds too late, that could have been the difference between her living and dying. This means that in all argumentative honesty I must look at my chosen course, judging its rightness or wrongness, as if the result had been Felicia's death that day. Murphy's Law, which we all like to joke about, in fact exists for very good reasons.

I am not trying to resolve anything here. Perhaps we could keep from throwing the baby out with the bathwater if we explored the fact, and its implications, that Felicia was under coercion by Pyotr, that her will was not entirely free. This was something to which I failed to give due consideration at the time. At any rate, I came to the jarring realization on the Tuesday after Labor Day that my own free-spirited approach to our relationship was an indulgence that Felicia could ill afford to partake of with me.

Let's proceed now toward Allen Bill Pond. How well do you know Calgary and environs, Reader? If you're quite familiar with it then you can skip the travelogue here and continue on wherever the edge-of-your-seat, action-packed thriller proper picks up again. On the other hand, if up till now it has remained outside your experience, then please lend me your ear and let me tell you about this beautiful jewel of a city which is mine, all mine.

Calgary is a glitter of crystal in a salad of green dropped where the foothills of the Rockies meet the prairie. The snow-tipped mountains form a backdrop so close that you can practically reach your hand out and touch their chilly peaks. From their glaciers flow the Bow and Elbow rivers, which join at the site where old Fort Calgary was built in the late eighteen-hundreds by the Royal Northwest Mounted Police to help maintain law and order, peace and quiet, in the surrounding region. You will find no newer and cleaner city on the face of the globe than Calgary, where even rats are barred entry and cockroach sightings make the local news. For those who love clear blue skies, vast parks, bike paths beside still waters — and gurgling, and hop-skip-and-a-jump access to genuine wilderness, genuine silence where the rasping wing-flap of a raven can be heard from hundreds of yards away, there is no need to search further, for here is paradise found.

I could tell you of the world-renowned beauty west of Calgary surrounding Banff and Canmore in the mountain parks. The vision known to us mortals as Lake Louise. The fortressy crags of Kananaskis. Elk patrolling majestically. Moose patrolling even more majestically, so very tall. Mountain goats dancing up and down sheer rock faces. The view from Mount Norquay. The view from its switchback, down which I am amazed the delinquent James Bond has yet to career in full flight. Mount Rundle. Lake Minnewanka. The Three Sisters. Johnson Canyon. I could tell you of all that, and more, in goriest of detail; but there are limits to how far off track I will let a tangent take me. I take quite seriously my duty as narrator to provide you, the reader, with the details, all the details, and nothing but the details pertinent to this particular little fabricated piece of fiction. So we will leave the vaunted beauty around Banff up the valley of the Bow and train our sights instead on the hidden treasures to be discovered up the Elbow.

Did I tell you about Elbow Falls yet, Reader? Felicia and I spent a late afternoon there on a warm day in June. That's where I lost my lovely blue silk jacket, forgot it draped on the branch of a pine tree, rather. I felt bad because it was a pretty coat. Felicia felt even worse because it matched my eyes so perfectly and she loved to see it on me. Oh well, c'est la vie! Elbow Falls is not far at all from the outskirts of Calgary, but you are already in the mountains there, not just the foothills. The river is flowing rapidly, then has to bend around a large out-crop of rock. As it comes around this, it suddenly finds itself dropping thirty or forty feet straight down in a spectacular roar. Very picturesque, pine and aspen forest to the riverbanks, even breath-taking.

A spot I always wanted to take Felicia to is the Ice Caves, a fair ways up Signal or Moose Mountain — I forget which name is right, even though I have hiked to its crest twice and looked from there at the toy skyscrapers off to the east that are the city core. She was too pregnant by the time we thought to go there and the approach to the caves involves an ascent of a steep scree slope. I would describe to you the beauty and splendor of the variegated ice formations to be found in these caves, except it would be dishonest of me, for the only time I entered them I was young enough that my friend and I gained far greater pleasure from allowing the rest of the boys' club troop to troop on ahead and then smoking them back out with a smoke bomb than any appreciation of the aesthetics of nature could have given us. So my personal experience of the Ice Caves extends only to the portico.

There are a hundred beautiful spots you can discover blindfolded up the Elbow from Calgary, and all so readily available. You just drive the fifteen or twenty minutes to Bragg Creek and proceed from there; or instead, take the Marquis of Lorne Trail west past Spruce Meadows and a few miles of farmland until you find yourself in a rugged wilderness of forest, mountain, valley and rushing water.

It was the seventh of September when Felicia and I got in my car and set out to spend the afternoon somewhere pretty. We had no specific objective. I vaguely planned to head out to the falls and then go a little further from there to wherever caught our eye. Nor did I myself have any specific objective. I had set my mind on doing the right thing, but I still wasn't sure what this was. As we drove, we talked about a million things, just as usual. Our fingers interlocked, sometimes me bringing her fingertips up to receive their tribute of feather kisses from my lips, sometimes her drawing my fingertips up to stroke against her cheek or hair, just as usual.

We had just passed an entranceway to a camp winding off through the trees when we broke out into the open, descending a slope into a valley. "Oh, look at that!" exclaimed Felicia.

In the river-bottom below us on the left side of the road was a small body of water surrounded by clusters of trees. The leaves on the aspens were all golden. I knew the spot well because I had picnicked there a couple times, the last time just the previous Thanksgiving. It is a large pond with an outlet flowing into the river forty or fifty yards from it. Between it and the river is a belt of trees and bush with all kinds of paths going here and there. You can walk all the way around the pond and stop and sit any place you like on the short grass along its banks wherever the trees do not come to its edge. You have to pick your way carefully on the stepping-stones when you cross its shallow outlet, but that's easy enough, especially if you don't mind a little splashing.

Seeing Felicia's enchantment with the scene before us, I slowed down as we were crossing the bridge over the river and made the turn here into Allen Bill Pond. It was a beautiful, blue-sky day, warm under a bright sun. The air was rich with forest all around.

But for three or four other small parties, Felicia and I had the place all to ourselves.

We got out of the car and wandered down to the water's edge. There was no hurry in our world. We had nothing more pressing to do for the whole afternoon than enjoy each other's company in the embrace of nature. We walked and talked, drinking in the scenery all around, our conversation encompassing everything and nothing. A fly fisherman was at the pond's edge with his rod and reel. To the left were strung a series of picnic sites, strategically located for privacy; a couple of these were in use. Eventually we meandered to the right, where no one was, to make our way around the pond and take a peek at the river hidden beyond it.

For the past couple days I had been wondering what I should do, turning things over and over in my mind. While I was satisfied with the rightness of my course to this point, there was no disputing its fundamental inadequacy as the reality of the situation had become more clearly revealed to me. Happily, I was under no pressure stemming from any really immediate urgency since Pyotr's staying in Houston for the next month provided a welcome respite for Felicia from any imminent danger. All the same, I'm not one for procrastination or time-wasting for no good reason. I had basically resolved on a new tack, quite at odds with the old one and with my own personal inclinations, but I had no firm ideas as to commencing with it, no plan whatsoever. I am too much of a believer in spontaneity, in melding with the current equilibrium to produce the future one, in joining in — not dictating — the dance that is life, to have had any real plan in hand.

As we strolled dreamily arm in arm around the pond, chattering aimlessly together, the sensation dawned on me that the conjunction of the planets was right and the time to proceed had come. I stopped Felicia, pecked her on the cheek and told her I had something important to say. She looked at me and smiled. "I love you," I breathed in her ear, as I pecked her cheek a second time. Looking deeply into her eyes, I took both her hands in mine, got down onto one knee and asked her to marry me.

Felicia started to cry.

Oh no! What had I done?! Here I had wanted to give my kochanie something good, properly provide her forever the protection and security she needed, and instead all I'd done was conflict yet again my dear little Catholic, and probably worse than ever.

"Don't cry, Felicia!" I jumped up. "I didn't mean to hurt you." The last thing in the world I wanted to do was hurt her. "I'm a thoughtless fool. Forget I said anything at all. Please don't cry." I pulled her close as I said this and pressed her to my breast, patting her head as she buried it in my shoulder. She was really crying hard. I felt so awful, so more-harm-than-good.

"Hush, silly!" she gasped through her tears.

We stood like that for a minute or two, Felicia gushing tears and me feeling remorseful and stupid for causing such a deluge, until finally she had brought herself under control. I tried again, "Forget I said anything, darling. I didn't mean to hurt you."

Felicia pulled back from my embrace and looked full in my face. Her cheeks were bathed in tears. Yet on her lips, in her eyes, was the most radiant, angelic smile you could ever possibly imagine.

"Garusz," Felicia said, in a tiny little voice, "I married you long ago."

Chapter 14

The month of September was our true honeymoon. Felicia and I spent it together in blissful relaxation, nothing to distract us from each other. We didn't do anything new and out of the ordinary — Felicia was too pregnant for adventure or unnecessary exertion. I took a beautiful picture of her resting with her eyes closed basking outside in the sun. She snapped some photos of me on a footbridge in the mountains wearing my favorite sunglasses and sporting a cute little ponytail, the longest my hair had been for three or four years. I gave her 'The Razor's Edge' and then read it to her, bit by bit, over a week or so. We took her son up to Banff on a Saturday and spent the whole day sightseeing and shopping. It was a pleasant, happy month. Though we were not ignoring or neglecting the future, we were eagerly gorging ourselves on the present.

The future. What to do about the future? What were we going to do? Where would we go from here? I didn't have two cents to rub together. That was no big deal to me, but it was less than reassuring for Felicia. Further, I was preparing to embark on another three or four years of studies, so there was no short-term prospect of my financial solvency. We were agreed that this was all for the best in the long run, but it did not help matters in the least for the near future.

I should take a moment here to explain about my proposed return
to university. It may come as a shock to you, Reader, after
having made myself out to be such an okay guy, such a decent
— or at least semi-decent — sort, to learn that I was preparing to
enter law school, readying myself to set out on the broad and
winding that would lead down, down, down till at last I would
wake up one day and find myself a lawyer, horns, pitchfork, tail
and all. It pains me to admit it, but there, in the name of full
disclosure, you have it. Think what you will. I cannot deny the
truth.

For a couple years or so prior to this time I had been batting
around the idea of law school. While working on a technology
project, I'd been compelled to put together a patent application
and this experience had brought me to the realization that
lawyerly pursuits were not all necromancy and human sacrifice
— or had the potential not to be so, at any rate. I found in myself
a certain facility with the law, which presented itself to me as a
series of puzzles, some simple and straightforward, some more
complex to varying degrees, all needing to be organized together
in the most logical, or most useful, way possible. Ironically —
and I say "ironically" because there really is so much wickedness
and self-serving manipulation in the practice of law — it was my
lifelong fixation with, worship of and pursuit after, truth that had

given me such an easy, intuitive grasp of the law, perception and truth being such close cousins. Anyhow, for some time I had intended in the back of my mind, barring the appearance of a better opportunity, to go to law school and secure for myself entrance to an interesting and well-remunerated vocation. In fact, the previous winter I had looked on my erstwhile summer trip to Europe as a last-ditch effort to seize a career in itinerant grape-picking or some other such bit of honesty, failing which I would resign myself to embracing the legal profession.

It was when it became apparent to me, in about February, I would not be spending the summer overseas, that I set the ball rolling towards getting myself into law school. Do you know, Reader, what is involved in getting enrolled? It is not a simple thing at all. First you have to have a degree. Then you have to take the Law School Admissions Test (LSAT), administered twice a year from some agency in Pennsylvania, I believe. Finally you have to locate a school that is willing, for whatever reason, to give you one of their hundred or so seats that enrollment over eighteen hundred or more ready and ruthless fellow applicants. It is a major undertaking to get into law school, and the majority of those who set out to do so must ultimately accept disappointment.

Already in possession of a degree (history, for your information), I determined to maximize my chances of doing well on the admissions test. Since this test is, more than anything, an IQ test, there is really very little you can do to enhance your eventual performance on it, notwithstanding what all the self-help books and courses try to claim. There is no special knowledge, no special area of knowledge, that will help you. You had better be able to communicate logically with a quick and easy comprehension. But as for studying, per se, forget it — and do not even think of trying to cheat! Anyway, here is how I approached it: The next testing session was set for June. In early March I got a couple self-help books from the library so as to access the series of full-length sample tests they contained. I also ordered some genuine tests given over previous years from the organizing agency in Pennsylvania. For about three months, each Saturday beginning at one in the afternoon and following precisely the official timing regime, I did my weekly test. In this way, I became thoroughly familiarized with all the various question formats and I programmed my mind to be most ready for such an exercise during that exact portion of the day. (The test in June was slated for the afternoon.) Whatever the actual benefit to me may have been is impossible to say; but I can tell you for certain that this methodology removed any aura of mystery from the actual test and gave me a definite confidence boost. I can also tell you that the genuine tests from Pennsylvania were much harder, and therefore more help to me, than the ones I got out of the books. (And in fact, my results on those genuine tests were all within two percentage points either way of my results on the real thing in June.)

So how did I do in June? Well. Well enough to balance out the fact that my marks from university identify me as someone who at the time considered it a challenge to his integrity to study for tests and therefore derive scores not reflective of his actual permanent gain in knowledge. Felicia accompanied me to the university at lunchtime that day — it may have been a Tuesday — and gave me a peck on the lips for luck as she left to get back to class. You do not need a blow-by-blow of the test itself, but I will tell you that the one experimental section inserted always into each of these tests scared the daylights out of me until I stepped back and realized what it was. By the time everything was wrapped up that afternoon it was getting on toward supper, so I just went home and called Felicia to let her know all had gone well. It was late July before I knew for sure the results.

You can see now that when Felicia and I were giving consideration in September to the future, our future together, we were both intent on making an accommodation for my study of law. The general idea was that I would choose a university in western Canada and begin classes the following September, so there was no big rush to get my applications out immediately as they would not be seriously reviewed until early spring. I was disinclined to remain in Calgary and enroll at my former university here because I felt it was better to earn a second degree at a different institution from the one that had awarded the first. All of this meant that my scholastic future was in a real state of limbo without even any geographical focus to orient ourselves around — I could have ended up in any of three or more cities, the three most likely being Edmonton, Vancouver and Victoria. This state of affairs was not helpful in the least as regarded Felicia's situation, yet neither she nor I thought it sensible or preferable for me to abandon the potential here for some more immediately lucrative pursuit. So there things stood, a fog of contingency and delay to further exacerbate my attempts at providing Felicia assistance. I did make an exploratory expedition up to the University of Alberta in Edmonton, hoping to get a strong enough — even if preliminary — indication to go ahead and establish myself in that city; however, I was disappointed to find that this school, a very good school other-wise, was unique in placing very little relative weight on the admissions test results in the mix of factors they considered for acceptance — so I could all but rule out this convenient solution to our need for direction.

Where did all this leave Felicia and me? In a state of confusion, disorientation. We talked about her leaving Pyotr, and us living together somewhere, but where? And providing for ourselves how? Without any foundation of practicality or context of stability, all our talk of a future together was more fantasizing than planning and preparation.

As September rolled along and the crisis of Labor Day faded from the forefront of our thoughts, Felicia and I both felt less and less urgency as to removing her from an abusive situation. Read this last sentence again, Reader, if you will, especially the latter part. It makes me stop here as I am writing and just shake my head. We "felt less and less urgency as to removing her from an abusive situation." I have given you a fair idea of the chronic abuse Felicia suffered. I described to you one of the worse assaults precisely as I remember her describing it to me — and it was horrific. And I have told you of a near miss, a very-near-miss, that could very well have resulted in the deaths of both Felicia and her baby. Good heavens! How abusive must a situation be for us, for me, for my society, to throw "practical" to the wind and simply extricate the victim from her peril without further ado? It was all such a tangle, but as I consider it now in hindsight, I can see how foolish I was to proceed, to attempt to proceed, in an unwavering mode of self-reliance. I should have swallowed my pride, acknowledged my inadequacy in dealing with a situation way out of my depth, and turned to the larger society for help — family, friends, the authorities, maybe even the church. Domestic abuse is a very difficult matter to tackle and society may yet be ill-equipped to do so very effectively, but very few solitary individuals are any better-equipped to effect satisfactory outcomes. Of course immediately following the Labor Day crisis I had proposed to Felicia that she seek safe haven in a women's shelter, but she was unwilling to give such an idea consideration, not surprisingly.

Toward the end of September there was a closing program for
our class. Studies had finished a month earlier and now
everyone's practicum had come to a successful end. Personally,
not being much of one for ritual and having become contentedly
sated with my level of acquaintance with the good people of our
class several months earlier in March or February (or late or
mid-January for that matter), I would not have bothered going.
However, Felicia wanted to go, so I readily relented. You should
have seen her that day, that evening. She was looking so divine,
eight months pregnant and all. (Sans lunettes, need I say?) She
was a sparkling blonde cascade, the fountain of all loveliness. I
was so captivated by her, so proud of her, so proud of "this
beauty by my side". And no, in case you wondered, Reader, I
never will forget the way she looked that night. Radiant. The
sun. My sun.

When the festivities were over and we had made our way back to
my car, Felicia suddenly suggested we take a walk on the
campus as the night was so pleasant and mild. But first she
wanted to get a bag out of the car. I knew something was up
because I hadn't seen her sneak any bag into my car when I'd
picked her up that evening. However my little sphinx was saying
nothing and making no invitation for inquiry. Knowing that all
would be revealed in the fullness of time, I kept my curiosity in

check, or at least my tongue. Once we'd retrieved this bag, we
strolled along at a leisurely pace with no particular direction in
mind until we found ourselves come to a pretty view. Nearby,
stalwart old Robert the Bruce silently kept his endless vigil over
my city.

"I have something for my kochania," Felicia said with a smile. I
pulled her into me and gave her temple a light kiss. Drawing a
package out of the bag, Felicia handed it to me and told me to
unwrap it. Holding this package in my hands, I guessed that it
contained a sweater. That was just the right weight and feel for
whatever was wrapped up inside. The pattern of the wrapping
itself was of large, flower-wreath hearts containing the words
'You are on the threshold of a lifetime of love.' I was touched,
smitten to the core, truth to tell, by the wrapping alone. How I
loved my darling Felicia! I kissed her on both brows just for the
wrapping. (I don't mean to foreshadow, but I'll tell you that, two
and a half months ago, when I found myself very abruptly setting
out traveling, and traveling light, nothing but the clothes on my
back and a walletful of money, the one and only thing I took
with me was one of these hearts torn hastily from the rest of the
wrapping. 'You are on the threshold of a lifetime of love.')

Never before in my life had I unwrapped a gift with any less
ferocity than a ravenous wolf or hyena might exhibit
(particularly if it smelled raw meat inside); never had I left a

119

gift's wrapping in any other state than shreds and tatters fit only for the fire. But not this time. No woman, no Scotchman, ever treated any gift-wrap with such tender, loving care as I bestowed on this. Slowly, ever so slowly, brain surgeon-slow, I peeled each bit of tape and removed or re-fastened it as necessity dictated. It wasn't easy, not with such soft contents, but I took my time and did my best.

At last, the delicate operation of unwrapping was complete; the moment of revelation had arrived. I was entirely prepared to tell Felicia what a beautiful sweater it was (she has excellent taste and an exquisite eye for color, so this would have been perfectly sincere, even if premeditated). I even had a thank you-for-the-lovely-sweater kiss all ready and waiting for her. But guess what? It wasn't a sweater. Instead, there in my hands was a beautiful potpourri, heart-shaped and made of delicate white lace. I loved it.

"I made two, kochania. One for you and one for me."

I laid a tender kiss on Felicia's lips. Then another. Then one more for good measure.

"And it is made of what, kochania?" She had a twinkle in her eye.
This was a little out of left field for me. Being a guy, I thought I

was doing well to be able to identify the cloth as lace – and just to know what a potpourri is, for that matter. I gave Felicia a baffled look.

"Kochania, my kochania," she looked deep into my eyes. "I used my wedding veil to make these potpourris." Her lips curled up mischievously. "Now you may kiss your kochanie again."

Reader, I beg you to tell me: Could there be any more romantic soul anywhere on the face of God's green earth than this, my dear, sweet Zuhdoethekaunee? I doubt it. I really, truly doubt it.

Chapter 15

It was the middle of October when Felicia had her baby, a beautiful baby boy. Both mother and child came through the ordeal of childbirth with the best of health, though Felicia was left rather exhausted and in need of a few weeks of rest for recuperation.

Pyotr came back to Calgary a few days before the baby was born. He had arranged a week off from work to be home with Felicia around the time of her due date. I was concerned for her that he might again be violent, and this at the most critical stage of all when she would be extremely vulnerable, but she assured me with complete confidence that there would be no trouble whatsoever. Pyotr had been away and lonesome for long enough that he would not have the slightest inclination toward brutality. She said that he would be good for at least a month and possibly much longer, depending on how much pressure he was coming under at work.

Pyotr may have been peaceful enough when he came home in October, but he was such a handful — he'd had little or no social outlet for the last four or five weeks — that within just a couple days he was driving Felicia up the wall with his constant need for attention. She soon begged me to get him out of the house for a few hours and give her a little break.

Just as all boys love firecrackers, so all men love firearms. This is something deep in the male psyche, as natural — almost as natural — as the attraction to the female form. Any man who says otherwise is in denial. No matter that he may have seen reason and supports the eradication of all firearms from human society, when a man sees a gun he wants to hold it in his hands and make it go bang. That is just the way it is. So when I'd mentioned to Pyotr earlier on, in the summertime, that I had an old shotgun, he had been eager to try it out sometime. Had it been the sort of outing where you can take along the whole family, or more specifically the wife, I would have been just as eager as Pyotr to see this urge of his gratified. As it was, I knew that taking him out shooting would mean spending a few hours with him without the pay-off of being together the whole time with Felicia. I may love loud noises just as much as any other juvenile of the gender, but that would have been asking a little too much of me. It was only when I saw my sweetheart needing a respite from his constant pestering and inanity that I decided to bite the bullet, as it were, and spend an afternoon alone with Pyotr. Accordingly, we planned out a little jaunt to somewhere remote west of Black Diamond.

The day Pyotr and I went shooting I lunched with him and

Felicia at their place before packing him off in my car to the hills. Felicia was not feeling like she would be giving birth that day, but she had Pyotr's rental car in case of anything urgent. I had no particular place in mind as we set out. I chose the mountains over the farm or ranch country because I didn't feel like introducing Pyotr to anyone I knew or knocking on farmhouse doors and begging farmers to trust a couple of city boys to run loose on their land with artillery. We drove until we found a logging road that beckoned and then followed it till we were deep in the forest miles from the nearest living soul.

There's little to tell of this day other than the obvious: We went. We saw. We shot. I had tossed a bag of plastic pop bottles, some full, in my trunk so we would have targets worthy of our skill level. Pyotr told me that he had served the obligatory year or whatever of military service in Poland in the late seventies or early eighties. If that was the case, he must have served in the tank corps or maybe logistics, because he sure didn't know how to handle a gun, how to keep from swinging the business end past yours truly.

When the day was drawing to a close — or more precisely, when we ran out of ammunition — and we'd satisfied our bloodlust, we gathered up the synthetic carnage and picked our way down the deer track we had ascended the quarter mile or so from where my car was tucked away in some trees. As we walked, Pyotr made a comment that saddened me terribly, made me sad for him, that is. He told me that, in all the eight or nine years since he had moved to Canada, this was the best day of his life here. He said this with all the candor and enthusiasm of a child, and he meant it. Why did his comment make me so sad for him? He had a beautiful wife and a loving six-year-old son born in Canada. He had a highly-paid, intellectually-stimulating position in a good company that was a leader in its field. To enhance his earning power as an engineer, he had pursued and completed his MBA three or four years earlier from a top university. He lived in a fine area with good neighbors. And this was the best he could do? Shooting pop bottles with his wife's lover, someone who was so totally not-there with him? What poverty! What deficiency of the soul! I felt genuine pity for this creature who had not a single friend in the whole world. He had made his own bed, but that's beside the point. And don't tell me that Pyotr was unaware of my relationship with Felicia: Deep down in his subconscious he knew plain as day where her heart lay; of that I was already convinced, which fact was all too painfully confirmed by later events. Pyotr was taking friendship where he could find it and the saddest thing about his comment that day was its very truth. His words were the words of a man who had forgotten long before what life is all about.

On the day Felicia's baby was born I had gone to a friend's place for supper and I didn't return home until fairly late. There was no message on my answering machine from Felicia and she hadn't called me at all earlier in the day, so I suspected that the baby had made his appearance at last. The next day it was all I could do to wait until lunchtime and then I called her number. Pyotr answered the phone and told me the good news. He said that all was well but Felicia was too worn out to want any company. I congratulated him on everything and confirmed that the hospital she was at was the Rockyview. After chatting for a little while, quite a while longer than I intended, I finally got the phone hung up. I then called the Rockyview to check their visiting hours and when the appointed time arrived I jumped in my car and sped down there.

A funny thing happened on my arrival at the hospital. I am very familiar with Calgary's hospitals, and especially their maternity wards, because for quite a few years I had delivered flowers to them each Mother's Day. However, the one hospital I did not know, had never set foot in that I can recall, was the Rockyview there in the southwest overlooking Glenmore Reservoir. So instead of just marching right in and making straight for the appropriate wing, I had to find the main desk and get directions and then muster all my mental reserves to ensure that I would be able to follow these directions successfully. (Are all hospitals the world over so confusingly laid out, or is this just a peculiarity of Calgary's?) Needless to say, it took me some time, and a re-direct or two, to locate the maternity ward, but this delay was a godsend. When I eventually got there all the nurses at the desk were busy and, after waiting for a minute, I just moseyed past and started to look for Felicia's room. At this point I heard a familiar voice. It was Pyotr. I really did not want to see him but if it was unavoidable then it was unavoidable. He was talking to a nurse. Whether I went backward or forward, I would run into him because the nurses' station was an island, the core of the wing, around which all the rooms were arranged. My mosey became a crawl. As the nurses' desk came into my view again, I could see Pyotr talking there, his back to me. (I had passed Felicia's room but had felt it best to deal with Pyotr first rather than have him walk in to find me with her.) Just as I approached him to say hello, and even as I was taking in that little pre-utterance half-breath we all take in as we are about to speak, Pyotr abruptly started to walk toward the exit hallway. I was close enough to take one step and touch his arm. Feeling confused as to what I should do, I held my tongue yet followed behind him ready to make a greeting. We walked like this for maybe ten paces to the exit, me being no more than five feet behind him. He even turned his head once and looked to the side. In those first few steps I was all indecision, wanting only for him to see me so that I could say a nonchalant hello and kid him for taking so long to notice me. But then, as the exit loomed, I was mentally shooing him out the door. Once he was out in the hall, I turned around and left him to visit Felicia. I was still shaking my head with the peculiarity of the experience as I entered her room and saw her.

Felicia was so happy to see me! She said she knew I would come. For my part, you know, Reader, that I was just as happy to see her. Happy to see her, to be with her, and happy to see with my own two eyes that she'd had her baby safe and sound, that her high-risk pregnancy had come to a conclusion without mishap. Her baby was asleep in a bassinet. I checked the little guy out and he looked every bit as cute as any baby should, ten fingers, ten toes, all that. Felicia was very pleased as she told me that he had blue eyes. It was her belief, and she had more than half-convinced me, that an expectant mother could affect her baby's eye color by gazing into eyes of the desired color for long stretches of time during pregnancy.

Not wanting to create unnecessary problems, political problems, I brought Felicia a good book instead of flowers and as I gave it to her I told her to tuck it away when she expected Pyotr to visit. My mentioning him put her into a flurry and she told me he'd just left and would be back shortly. Apparently he had had to take care of some paperwork downstairs and he would return for a while before leaving the hospital. I was none too pleased to think that I would have to end up sharing some time with him after all this day, but it was no big deal to me either.

At that point, Felicia informed me of the latest developments with Pyotr. "Garusz, he has become very jealous and suspicious. He is worried that the baby is not his. You cannot let him find you here. He does not want you to visit me. He says that if you visit me here that will be proof of all his suspicions. This would ruin all our plans for you to come see me in Houston. He would never allow that if he were to catch you here with me now."

What Felicia was referring to regarding our plans for me to see her in Houston was the trip we had arranged two months earlier that would re-unite us for a three-week visit soon after she would have made the move south. It wasn't three days after Pyotr got word of his impending transfer before Felicia and I found a seat sale to Houston and saw a travel agent to arrange my flight. That was in August. My clever darling subsequently took her time over the following weeks and got Pyotr to the point where it was his idea that I visit them in Houston. I was then officially invited and supposedly booked my flight. As you can imagine, in all the turmoil and confusion over the two months since we had made these plans, there was often enough doubt in our minds whether even Felicia herself would be going to Houston. However, I had the ticket and as September flowed into October we had increasingly reverted to viewing the future in a Houstonian context.

Hearing Felicia's words, I shared her sense of alarm and after a few quick words of my own in parting, I took my leave of her.

The only danger zone lay in the few paces from her room past the nurses' desk to the nearest stairwell. I casually traversed this in no time flat and then took the stairs all the way to the basement parking lot where my trusty steed was waiting to speed me off.

Chapter 16

What was I doing thinking of going down to Houston? Well, boys and girls, this is a perfect example of the happy-go-lucky, take-it-as-it-comes outlook on life. I had no clear-cut vision of the future, or program to impose on it, but I had a simple, unwavering faith in its benevolence. One way or another, whether I be proacting or reacting, everything would turn out just dandy. (And I will confess to you, Reader, that in spite of all the difficulties I have encountered lately, I have yet to lose this simple faith that the future shines with goodness, shines brilliantly so, for me and mine.)

When Felicia and I planned in August my trip to see her in November, the scope of our intentions did not extend at all beyond that visit. We wanted to be together at any and every opportunity, and we certainly did not want to allow any possibility for the bond between us to break or wither away; but as for any long-term projections or objectives, those were outside our means, practically-speaking, and if we discussed them at all it was only in the form of daydreaming out loud. We had already spent a half year together in a most unorthodox relationship and enjoyed every minute of it. Neither of us felt any pressing need to subside from where we were into conventionality. It was only the necessity of meeting Pyotr's brutality with a sustainable alternative situation for Felicia that ended up forcing our thinking to develop along such lines a little later on, in the beginning of September.

For the last couple weeks of October Felicia and I were free once again from Pyotr's intrusiveness as he was back at work in Houston. Not that we particularly took advantage of this freedom. Or should I say, not that we were able to take advantage of it. A newborn is a twenty-four-hour-a-day job. Add to that Felicia's busyness with preparations for the move south and the fact that her labor in childbirth had been taxing enough that it was a good five or six weeks before she was finally feeling herself again, and you can see that our final weeks together in Calgary were hardly the most romantic. I helped her as much as I could to get everything organized and we did a lot of running around taking care of a million little errands. That's how the latter part of October passed. Pyotr returned at the very end of the month to escort Felicia and the children back to Houston and a couple days later I saw them off at the airport. It would be a matter of only two weeks until my kochanie and I would be together again, but I don't have to tell you, Reader, that those two weeks went by very sloooooooooowly.

It was a Sunday morning when I flew out of a chilly Calgary on my way to Houston. The flight was pleasant — I love flying —

with a bit of delay in landing as there had been a late morning thunderstorm in Houston. We circled the city a few times before coming in to land and I got a chance to see what an enormous sprawl it is. Houston must be forty miles across. One edge of it would come into view beneath us and I would watch and watch and watch as suburb after suburb rolled by; it felt like a good five or ten minutes until the other edge would finally appear — a long time in a jet, even coasting along at reduced speed. I was really impressed by all the trees I could see, both their numbers and size. Upon my arrival, I found Pyotr waiting for me and we drove for almost an hour before reaching his and Felicia's new home in a bedroom community still under construction five miles or so beyond the western edge of the city.

Reunited, Felicia and I. You can imagine how we felt. Of course we were restrained that first day with Pyotr present. As sister leading brother, my darling gave me a tour of the house and showed me to the room that would be mine for the next three weeks. It was a nice house, but I'm afraid I hardly noticed since my thoughts were elsewhere, as were Felicia's. I could feel the palpitation of her heart every time I looked into her eyes. I hardly dared spare her a glance that day lest she betray herself, or I myself, for that matter. However, we were able to keep our amorous thoughts in check until the following morning when Pyotr was gone to work and Felicia had seen her son off to school on the school bus.

Felicia and I spent that whole first week just luxuriating in each other. I am tempted to say that we spent the entire week in each other's arms, as that is my predominant memory of it, but we actually got a measurable amount of work done each day as well. It was kind of important for us to perform these daily labors because the whole pretext for my visit was to help Felicia get settled into her new home. So, between bouts of unbridled intimacy, we engaged in a kaleidoscope of more productive activities such as rather intimate shelf-hanging, rather more intimate closet-stuffing and particularly intimate wallpapering. We did a lot of that wallpapering. Or maybe it's more accurate to say that we put a lot of time that week into wallpapering. We got the kitchen done, as I recall, with a border, no less — partly done, anyhow.

That first week of my visit passed by so quickly that at its conclusion the following Sunday both Felicia and I were struck by how tragically brief a period of three weeks can be. My coming departure, even though twelve or thirteen days down the road, suddenly loomed large in our minds and only grew larger from that point onward. Starting then, our focus shifted from the present back to the future. We still had a lot of wallpapering to do, mind you, and we continued to devote ourselves to it most vigorously, it and all the other things, but now we began to scramble in earnest to conjure up a practical plan for the future that would keep us together.

Back in Calgary in September, when it had seemed imperative that Felicia leave Pyotr immediately, the most viable course of action we could come up with was for the two of us to work together in building and running a small cafe. That would have worked out okay with my studies. I had a close and reliable connection in Calgary who had offered in the past to guide me in establishing and managing such a business, and who could help me do so even with my limited means. Felicia and I could have pursued such an enterprise anywhere in western Canada and it would have been successful, providing us with a decent if not extravagant income. The fact is that, had I been able to pin down in September which city to build in, we would almost certainly have gone ahead with this at that time and Felicia wouldn't have made the move to Houston. As things stood, however, there was no possibility of proceeding on it for the next six months or more, so we had to shelve, or at least backburner, the plan.

It was in that second week of my visit to Houston, while the two of us were enjoying a croissant together at a trendy little restaurant, that Felicia revived this eatery idea with a new twist: Why not do it in Houston? I could take my schooling there just as well as any place else. This modified plan had a certain appeal, in spite of various difficulties it entailed. There was a substantiality it possessed that was lacking in all our other possibilities: it was a plan that we could begin testing and pursuing virtually without delay. Moreover, if we were to proceed with it, there would be no extended period of separation keeping the two of us from each other, and most importantly, whatever security I was able to provide Felicia would be available to her sooner this way than any other way. I liked the idea enough that after we batted it back and forth for a couple days I started calling around to do some basic research on local law schools, on the one hand, and possible eatery locations, on the other. The results of this preliminary research proved to be quite promising: There were two law schools in Houston, both of which expressed strong interest in my application. And there were scads of promising locations for a small cafe available at rates significantly lower than the going rates in Calgary. I decided to go ahead and pursue this course, and from that point on I devoted myself to it resolutely.

Meanwhile, Felicia and I had gotten that house of hers wallpapered within an inch of its life. That might be a slight exaggeration. We had finally finished the kitchen, anyway. It amazes me to think back now of how long it took us to do so precious little. I could have done that kitchen by myself in a single day. By the second weekend it was becoming clear to Felicia that our work output together was seriously deficient and she began to worry that we wouldn't get the other main wallpapering project, the master bath, done before I had to leave. Therefore, after supper on the Saturday we set out on a marathon wallpapering binge — and I mean strictly the hanging of wallpaper, no extracurricular distractions, not with Pyotr present. (Felicia invited him to participate, but he cleverly declined.) I don't know what time we started that evening, maybe six or seven. I expected to finish by eleven or so. After all, it was a small enough room. But, you know how those small rooms with a thousand irregularities to go around can be when you are painting, Reader. The same applies for wallpapering. It was past four in the morning when we finally finished, and a wastefully chaste four in the morning it was with our chaperone at hand.

Pyotr. The ever-present shadow. For those first two weeks of that visit he had been the perfect Polish host. But come Sunday morning he was in a foul mood. The previous night's wallpapering had disturbed his sleep. Then Felicia slept late, so his breakfast was delayed. I was awake but still upstairs when I heard a really loud crash downstairs. I jumped up to head down there and see what was going on, but then I heard the baby crying and Felicia's voice soothing him. She was on her way up the stairs. She didn't tell me all the details till later, but what had happened was Pyotr had gotten angry waiting so long for breakfast and he had thrown a large metal pot down on the kitchen floor. No damage had been done and he hadn't followed this up with physical violence against Felicia, but the loud noise and disturbance had made the baby cry. When I went down a few minutes later, Pyotr didn't seem embarrassed in the least by his outburst, though neither of us mentioned anything about it.

Observing Pyotr in that final week of my visit, my concern for
Felicia's safety was only heightened further. He frequently
exhibited ill-temper and rudeness toward her. She excused and
explained all of this away by telling me that he was feeling
particular pressure at work that week and this was his way of
coping. He was preparing for an important business trip the
following week, which in itself was part of a major project he
was working on, and the two together, the trip and the project,
occupied his mind constantly. Be that as it may, nothing justified
what I was seeing that week, the worst of which was an actual
case of assault by any legal standard.

On the Tuesday or Wednesday night, Felicia was working on
something in the kitchen and I was sitting at the table looking for
some number in the phonebook. Pyotr walks into the room with
a handful of letters and asks Felicia where the prepared cheques
are to pay all these bills. She says she hasn't gotten around to
writing them up yet, ready for him to sign, that she will get them
all done up tomorrow. With that, simply that and nothing else, he
loses it. He starts screaming at her, using the filthiest language
you can imagine. Now, words — even the harshest of words —
are one thing, but what Pyotr did next was in that whole other
category. Felicia is standing facing him and behind her is the
kitchen counter and the window, the window with its Venetian
blind being about three or four feet from her back. He throws the
whole packet of letters in her face with such force that the ones

that miss her hit the blind hard enough to make it bounce around. I jump up, expecting to have to intervene. Pyotr turns to me and yells for me to go upstairs, telling me this is none of my business. He was wrong there, of course, even apart from the fact that I felt a special responsibility as to Felicia's well-being. He had just made it my business. Having witnessed an assault, I had a moral, and I believe legal as well, obligation to either put a halt to it myself or alert the authorities so they could sort things out. So I stayed where I was and said simply that I would not be leaving the room unless and until I was sure there would be no trouble between the two of them. Some tense moments followed, but Pyotr eventually got himself under control and promised me there would be no further violence. After a confirmation glance from Felicia, I left them alone and went upstairs ready to race back down if I heard things getting out of hand. A few minutes later Pyotr came to me, somewhat sheepishly, and apologized that I'd had to see that, explaining to me that Felicia sometimes really tried his patience. My intervention didn't seem to bother him.

The night I flew out of Houston was a Friday. Pyotr was off on his business trip the following afternoon. Had he not been departing so soon after, I don't believe I could have left Houston without making contact with the authorities or a women's shelter to try to arrange some sort of protection for Felicia. Pyotr's mood the whole week was, from what I could see, that vile.

Felicia, like many abuse victims, resolutely maintained her resistance to seeking outside help. She assured me that it all stemmed from Pyotr's pre-business trip pressure, and that in the few hours between my departure and his he would be too busy to beat her. Then, after his trip, he would be meeting her in Poland where they would spend a couple weeks with their families. So I left Houston with a ton of misgivings, feeling like I'd done little more than apply a band-aid which now needed to be replaced, and wondering if and how I would be able to apply the next one.

Chapter 17

Reader, you begin to see now what a tangle it all was. (And I am only hitting the high points, mostly from my own perspective. You are getting just a taste — I hope I'm giving you that, at least — of each dish, each main dish.) Life is not like the movies where it's clear-cut at all times exactly what Dudley Do-right should be doing and how he should be doing it. I came back to Calgary and spent the next three weeks looking in the mirror. The mirror that is the blue sky, or the star-filled sky, or a view of the mountains, or a pensive gaze into those eyes I have never seen but know so, so well.

What was I doing? What should I be doing? Was I taking my relationship with Felicia seriously? Should I be taking it seriously? Forget the word "seriously." How should I be taking it? Perceiving it? I had asked Felicia to marry me, for heaven's sake! Had I meant it? She had accepted. Had she meant it? Or were we just fantasizing, playing games with ourselves and with each other?

Do you know, Reader, I would never have proposed to Felicia had it not been the most natural thing in the world, the most natural step to take. I hate ritual, the ritualization of relationships and their definition, the conscious attempt to develop friendship, which is something best, most fully, developed unconsciously (just like breathing). Had Felicia and I not already been well beyond the point of marriage, so that our engagement in it was merely an acknowledgement rather than a projection, my proposal to her would have been a betrayal of my ideal of love, something I could not and would not have done.

Try as I might, ponder, poke and pry as I might, I could find no insincerity in our relationship, no insincerity in our respective approaches to our relationship, neither in Felicia's nor in mine. That she remained with Pyotr presented not the least difficulty to me in this respect. That was simple inertia. Her upbringing in communist Poland had conditioned her to the quiet and patient toleration of all manner of persecution; it had also taught her to value economic security far more highly than we in the Western world can really comprehend without having lived under such an oppressive regime. Besides all that, Pyotr used fear, raw physical fear, to keep her under his heel. He frequently threatened to kill her if she ever tried to divorce him. Felicia told me about these threats of his and I can verify their existence myself because on at least three occasions I heard them uttered by him in all seriousness. Keeping in mind that threats are mere words, and normally empty enough words at that, if any man is the type to end up killing his wife — and tragically, some men are — then few are moreso, more the type, than this man. That I did not press Felicia to leave him, in spite of all the good reasons for doing so, was simply my acknowledgement of my own inadequacy to provide her the economic and physical security that would be necessary in such a context.

It was hard, really, really hard, to know what was the best course here to pursue. However, the one thing I did know, about which I had not the least doubt, was that there wasn't the slightest bit of immorality in our duplicitous treatment of Pyotr. This was pure Cold War. He used all his powers of brutality to oppress Felicia and keep her on her knees. If we had to resort to artifice to secure her safety, then God bless artifice. The angels were on our side, even if they weren't making themselves overly useful.

Reaffirming in my own mind all of this may have afforded me some comfort with my actions and course up to that point, but it sure didn't give much guidance for the future. I was resolved to do my best to establish myself in Houston so as to be close enough to Felicia to provide her what protection and emotional support I could; but there were so many obstacles, the most obvious of which were that I'm not an American and I had no money. All the same, I gritted my teeth and determined to overcome the difficulties. I had a very specific minimum objective, and that was to set up a "safe house", a place of refuge where Felicia could run to in an emergency and get away from Pyotr. Even if I failed in my aim to remain there in Houston to be near her, at least I could maintain such a refuge to deal with the worst crises.

In the week between my return to Calgary and Felicia's traveling to Poland we were on the phone a lot. As it turned out, she did not receive a beating before Pyotr left on his business trip, just as she had predicted. However, she admitted that it had been nip and tuck; and, had Pyotr been given just a little more leeway timewise, she figured she would have paid in full for the work stress he was feeling.

It was the first week of January when I returned to Houston with a friend of mine who was willing to consider investing in my projected cafe. We spent a few days running around the city looking at possible sites, talking to realtors and crunching numbers. It was a very productive trip and we settled on a site that had incredible potential. It was in a brand-new mall just a few blocks from River Oaks, the poshest area of Houston. There were three universities within a very few miles. And, best of all, the space right next door to the cafe slot was a twelve-plex (duodecimaplex, I guess I should say) cinema. It really was the sweetest site imaginable and a child could have run a successful eatery out of it. The realtor viewed our bid favorably; and, even though a national chain had a contract for the space, that particular chain was experiencing rough times and there was no doubt that it would be ours with just a little juggling if the property's owner accepted our bid.

That trip was a really rushed trip. I spent what time I could with Felicia. I don't remember how much I'd told my friend about her, but obviously it was enough that he wasn't entirely in the dark. Felicia loved the site we had chosen as much as we did and she helped us make a video detailing it and the neighborhood round about. My friend and I then returned to Calgary and waited for word from the realtor on our bid.

It was at this time, in January as I awaited word from the realtor, that a distraction arose to fill my mind, a distraction to which no sane person could have possibly turned a blind eye. In the months since my LSAT results were released I had received a number of solicitations from various law schools. None of these had particularly impressed me and I was not even tempted to respond to them. However, on the eve of my January trip to Houston I had received another one, and this one was from Columbia Law School. I had looked twice at the return address, thinking it must be some third tier school from Oregon or South Carolina capitalizing on a good name, but it was the real McCoy. With the hustle and bustle of my approaching trip I just tucked this away in the back of my mind to consider more fully upon returning.

So when I got back to Calgary and had the chance to thoroughly mull over this latest offer, there was no escaping the conclusion that it was something I could not, in all good conscience toward myself, ignore. I talked to some of my former professors about it, and some lawyers too, and their unequivocal response, each and every one of them, was that this was a rare opportunity which should be pursued with all vigor. I agreed with them entirely. Who could disagree? My problem was focus, priorities. I was willing — eager — to pursue this possibility (and I should stress that it was only a possibility of enrollment, no guarantees), but not if such pursuit would lead me to neglect Felicia's plight.

Imagine, Reader, that you are a parent with a young child entering Grade One, and for some nightmarish reason you're forced to send the child to a school where there is constant violence of all degrees. How would you feel each morning as you sent your child off to school? How would you feel throughout the day as it slowly wore on, hour by dragging hour? And how would you feel each night as you tucked your child into bed knowing that another morning was just a few blinks away? Please stop reading for a moment and really think about it... That's something like how I felt regarding Felicia in her situation. I could hardly have cared for her more, felt more anxiety on her behalf, if she were my own child. No matter how much I enjoyed the physical passion we shared together, that end of things was nothing compared to the love I felt for Felicia the person; and I would've traded it all in a pinch for the assurance

148

that she would no longer be in danger — if such a fantastical trade were possible.

I returned to Houston at the end of January. This time I drove my car there. My plan was to finalize the deal on the cafe space and then play it by ear from there: if I could go ahead immediately and get the business under development, then I would stay in Houston and just take a quick one- or two-day trip to New York to deliver my application to Columbia and give it a helping hand; but if it would be a month or more yet till I could take possession of the space, then I would drive to New York and triangulate my way back to Calgary. My planning was predicated on the assumption that the cafe deal would be approved, of which I was quite confident. The national chain had told the realtor they would be happy to surrender their option on the space. My friend's and my proposal may have been a little rushed, but our fundamentals were solid and the realtor was optimistic the property owner would accept our bid. You can see then that I was surprised, almost shocked, to learn that in fact he rejected it.

I was with Felicia dropping off my applications to the two local law schools when I got a hold of the realtor and heard the disappointing news. I had been pestering him fairly constantly that day for word. This hit Felicia as hard as it hit me. Harder, actually — much harder. She had taken it on faith when I had reassured her that this cafe deal would be a go. If I was her lifeline, then the cafe was the lifeboat carrying me. She was despondent for the rest of the day, what part of the day we could share. She was like a crumpled little doll. I tried to tell her that it would all turn out okay, that there's more than one way to skin a cat, but nothing I said could raise her spirits that afternoon. I held her in my arms, stroked her hair and gave her a million kisses, but I couldn't perk her up. As we parted, she looked sorrowfully up into my eyes and said, "Garusz, I do not think I will ever see you again." And she believed it too, she really believed it.

I went back to my motel and spent the evening deep in thought. I had intended to drive off to New York in the morning. What Felicia had said was wrong. Or was it? I would return. Or would I? The more I thought about it all, the more this became a God or Mammon moment in my life, perhaps the most momentous point in my entire life. Did I think I would return to Felicia? Yes. Did I expect to return to her? Yes. Did I know I would return to her? Well... I know human nature. And I know, all too well, just how human I am.

I still can't decide whether I'm a fool or a sap, or worse. (What could possibly be worse than a sap?!?) But I can tell you one thing, Reader: This fool, this sap, can hold his head up and knows he will always be able to. I stayed in Houston.

Chapter 18

What's a Canadian without two cents to rub together (not even two cents Canadian) to do in an American city two thousand miles from home? Well, if he's a fool — and in the current case I think we have established this with a reasonable degree of certainty, then he will heed the call of his credit cards and relax into their gentle, loving arms. I had a lot of credit cards, a lot of glitter to relax into.

The first thing I did was get an apartment. I don't think I could have ended up with a better place if I had put in a custom order for it. This apartment was on Westheimer at Dairy Ashford, which put it about a fifteen-minute drive from Felicia's home. Yet it was a good mile beyond any routes Pyotr would travel with much frequency. The complex it was in was gated with twenty-four-hour security guards; nobody could drive in without knowing the security code or calling from the gate for clearance. And, as icing on the cake, the suite itself was nice, the neighbors were quiet, the grounds were landscaped beautifully (in a semitropical style), and the facilities included a well-kept pool area and gym. All in all, it was ideal and fit admirably my fundamental requirement of providing Felicia somewhere secure to run to.

Knowing that Keynesian economics are less workable, less
sustainable, on the individual level than the governmental, my
next objective was to develop an income. My first plan was to
take the technology project I've been working on intermittently
over the last few years and try to raise a little funding for it there
in Houston. This was not unreasonable as there were a number of
companies in that city that would be potential users of the
technology upon its full development. Since I hold a strong
patent covering this technology, an investor's investment in it
would carry a fair amount of protection. I hoped to raise enough
money so that I would be free to dedicate myself to the project
full-time until classes would begin in August, and then part-time
after that (though I hoped to bring it to fruition by summer
anyhow). Although I made some good contacts among the prime
suspects, one of whom looked briefly as if he was going to come
through with the funding, this ended up going nowhere and I
didn't feel I could afford the luxury of extending my efforts to
the higher-hanging fruit. Enter Plan B.

Actually, at this point there was no Plan B, precisely-speaking. I
just initiated a bunch of parallel efforts, one of which was bound
to come home to roost (if you don't mind me crossbreeding the
metaphor). I still pursued the technology thing. I applied for a
job or two. I considered throwing together a little tree-trimming
business, something I'd done quite profitably before in Calgary.
I talked to a couple business brokers, one of whom got mad at

me because I (quite stupidly) blabbed a little too freely to the employees of a business up for sale that I visited. And I gleaned some substantial leads out of the business classifieds of the local newspaper.

The result of all this parallelism was one Canadian, namely me, gaining ownership of one lovely little gift shop well-situated in a good strip mall on the southeast edge of Houston. Was I lucky? Indeed, I was. This was a tremendous opportunity. The former owners, fine people originally from a foreign country, had had a very advantageous location here, but they weren't making a go of it and the two reasons for this were plain to perceive. First, they specialized in collectibles, high-end collectibles, which is all well and good in the right setting, but the surrounding area here was middle-of-the-road middle class and provided scant demand for such offerings. And second, they often cooked meals in the backroom using pungent spices in the process, so that there was a pervasive, most-ungiftshoplike smell throughout the place that limited the browser's attention span to forty-second forays between air runs. I knew I could turn this flagging enterprise into a goldmine.

What a big job it is to turn a flagging enterprise into a goldmine! The landlord was an excellent man to deal with. He had a good property anchored by a drugstore toward one end and a grocery store toward the other, both being outlets of major national chains. In between, and on either end, all the spaces were filled with good, solid small businesses of the regular, strip mall variety, all except the space the landlord designated as gift shop space. Since he really wanted to keep a gift shop in this slot so as to maintain a good balance to his mall, he was motivated to give me various concessions within reason to insure that I could get the business going on a viable footing. That helped me out a lot, gave me some breathing room to rebuild the clientele.

After the paperwork between the landlord and myself was done up, I began by ordering all kinds of merchandise from a myriad of suppliers. This was before I took possession of the space. On March 1, the old owners vacated the place and I shut the store down for renovations. I really had no choice about closing it. At first I was to pay a certain amount for the old merchandise, the bulk of it, and have that to build on, but the old owners decided instead to move it all to the store of a relative of theirs. That was fine with me. Clean slate and all. I closed the place for three weeks and renovated it extensively while my pile of arriving merchandise slowly grew.

Reader, you are probably wondering what sort of gift shop expertise I was bringing to my new acquisition. Well, it's like this... none, really. What I was bringing, though, was the two-part Garian approach to small business. Part One says that ninety-nine percent of business success (or any other success in life, for that matter) is hard work and determination. I have seen simpletons, rank imbeciles, succeed where wise men fear to tread, and it's all because of these two things. If I ever had to choose between backing a determined dummy or a genius distracted by all manner of potential risk, all else being equal I would take the dummy over the genius any day. Part Two of the philosophy says that the point of a business (most businesses, anyhow) is to get people's money. Whatever you do, keep focused on getting that money. You might be the spiffiest-looking, purdiest-smelling auto mechanic this side of the Arctic Ocean, for instance, but if all that grooming distracts you from fixing cars and getting the attendant money, then you've lost your proper focus. Whatever goods or services your business provides, make sure to offer them in the most money-getting way possible. This is a simple maxim with wide-ranging implications: Treat your customers courteously and you will likely get their money in the future too; but be rude to them now, and guess what happens? Give your customers a good product and you will get their money; but give them something shoddy, and again guess what happens? Just always keep in mind: business is all about money. Get the money. Work hard and get the money.

For the first three weeks of my store's existence under new ownership, it was not getting any money whatsoever. That was okay though. It was getting ready to get money. I fixed the walls and painted them a nice light peach with some green here and gray there for contrast or highlighting. I installed a pile of slot-board and re-fixtured the place to a pretty considerable extent. I would have liked to replace the carpet, but that was beyond my means for the time being. I settled with cleaning it thoroughly and arranging runners to cover the worn areas. And I arranged all the incoming merchandise to the best effect possible, stretching it somewhat to make the place appear full even though half the stuff had not yet arrived.

What I possessed on March 21, the first day of spring, when I held my petite opening — the grand one could come later when I had more merchandise — was a good-looking gift shop newly renovated with extensive signage. It was in an excellent, high traffic, high-visibility location sandwiched between two busy anchors and situated in a good neighborhood comprising a fair-sized territory. I was starting out on a good footing, that was for sure. It was now up to me to manage the business well and fine-tune it into optimum performance and profitability.

One of the first things I learned was that people wanted to order invitations from a gift shop. Not being a woman or the sort of guy who might normally get into the gift shop business, I never had the slightest clue about this highly lucrative end of things. But, believe you me, once I twigged onto it, I found out all I could as fast as I could. The result was that I had catalogs from a selection of the premier invitation supply houses rushed out to me in time to snag a few graduation orders and a late spring wedding or two. The mathematics of this segment of my business was so advantageous to my bottom line that I made a point of placing ads in all the half-dozen or so yellow pages directories in the near vicinity specifically promoting this service; these ads were to come out in September and October.

The next thing I learned was that the selection and stocking of cards is as difficult as it is important. I got a whiff of this lesson on April Fool's Day, but it was Mother's Day when it really hit home hard. My approach in the first place had been to get a wide selection of cards from a lot of companies so that my store would have an interesting assortment beyond what was usually available. The previous owner had stocked cards from one of the two big national companies, but I resisted continuing with that on the grounds that such fare was blasé. I was wrong there. The big guys know what sells; moreover, in suburbia, in stripmallia, for every "interesting" person there are twenty regular Joes (Janes, actually — men do not buy cards), and so I had to tailor my wares to these Janes since that was where I would be getting the money from. When I ran out of Mother's Day cards two days before Mother's Day and had to send my (MY!!!) customers to the drugstore or the grocery store by the dozen to get cards to go with their gifts (tears rolling down my cheeks as I waved goodbye to each and every one of them), I knew the time had come to call in the cavalry. In all ways, going with a big card company was the best solution: I would get the bestselling selection of cards; I would get the right amounts of cards, and emergency supplies if needed; and I would no longer have to go through boring catalogs of cards upon cards upon cards to choose which ones to stock. In mid-June the company I went with came in with a hundred feet or so of cards. That alone soundly established the card segment of my business (and finally fleshed out the inventory so that the store no longer looked stretched a little thin).

There were other details of the store I had to tinker with to maximize its money-gettingness, but the two mentioned above were the most important. The numbers had always been a tad lower than I had projected, yet the rate of revenue growth had increased exactly as predicted right through the middle of May, and that was the most critical aspect. I had been warned by the previous owners that the customer traffic would dry up through the scorching summer when people fled to the enclosed malls, so the drop-off in late May and June didn't come as any big surprise. I was confident that by the time August and September rolled around my store would be humming along in high gear. And I still believe that, had not other events intervened so drastically, such would have been the case. But I'm getting ahead of myself. I really only intend to describe my gift shop business up until late May when Felicia left Houston for a summer visit to Poland.

GARY WILSON

Chapter 19

Felicia. After that last chapter, Reader, you must be wondering if I had entirely forgotten about her as I got going hard on my gift shop. Not at all.

When I called Felicia the day after we had parted (with her thinking she would never see me again) and told her I'd decided to remain in Houston, she was delighted and relieved. She was also instantly worried for me as to how I would support myself. I was equally worried on this score, of course, but I tried not to let on.

Something else that worried both Felicia and me was Pyotr, the thought of Pyotr accidentally bumping into me there in Houston. Such an encounter would have been disastrous. It was imperative that I avoid anything like this. Toward that end Felicia briefed me thoroughly on where not to be when. In addition, I had my locks shorn and got her to help me dye what remained blond. That way, if the unthinkable happened and I ran into Pyotr somewhere, hopefully he wouldn't recognize me and trouble would be averted.

Felicia and I spent all the time together that we could manage under the new circumstances. As I pursued some means of establishing an income, I kept her abreast of my efforts and progress. It was fortuitous that the business I ended up in was a gift shop — I would have taken anything that would hold body and soul together — because that was something that Felicia could really work together with me on. Not that it was practical for her to actually join me physically at the shop premises; it was a full hour's drive there one-way from her house, and on only a couple occasions when my manager — a real treasure, that lady was — couldn't make it in to cover for me did I get Felicia to come and keep the place running. How she really helped me out and contributed to the well-being of my store was, first, by meticulously going through hordes of supplier catalogs and advising me on the items that would sell (I would have been lost, clueless and bored to distraction without this assistance); and second, by making a huge assortment of dried flower arrangements and potpourris for me to sell, which not only brought in welcome revenue, but also gave my sparse inventory a much-needed boost.

In the first few weeks of living there in Houston, it was far easier for me to get together and spend time with Felicia than after I took over the gift shop. (Fortunately, by then it had become apparent to Pyotr that living five miles or so from the nearest bus stop made a one-vehicle household entirely unworkable and he had broken down and purchased a second vehicle.) Felicia and I mostly relaxed at my place where we had total peace of mind behind the walls and gated entry or, if she had some shopping to do, I would accompany her. Only on a very few occasions did we go back to her place; the risk in doing that was obvious. Once my labors at the gift shop began, my hours there were so long every day during the first six or eight weeks that we had to settle for seeing each other for only a few minutes, maybe an hour, on the odd morning. That situation pleased neither of us any too well, but we had to put up with it until the store was running smoothly and I felt I could hire staff.

Despite all the measures taken to keep Pyotr unaware of my presence in Houston, the one nagging concern that never escaped me was my car. A maroon Thunderbird is hardly anonymous, especially one with Alberta plates in Texas. If I were to overtake and pass Pyotr on a road, or he were to overtake me, the probability of him noticing and recognizing my car was too high altogether. The odds of such an occurrence happening might be fairly low in and of themselves, but they were there all the same; and the greater the period of time they were brought into play, the greater the risk that the crucial binary representing Pyotr's state of knowledge would switch from the benign to the catastrophic.

February went by with no problem. Same with March. It was in the latter part of April that disaster very nearly overtook me, or should I say, allowed me to overtake it.

On the day in question Felicia, prudent as always, had warned me that she and Pyotr would be downtown in the late afternoon. This meant that they would be traveling home on the same freeway, in the same direction, as I would normally have been on that day when I returned home from work. Consequently, I adjusted my routine a little and delayed my evening commute by about an hour. I might as well not have; that would have worked out better. Just as I came roaring past the city core and branched off the north-south artery onto the east-west one, what did I see but, lo and behold, a dark blue Nissan mini-van poking along a few car-lengths ahead in the lane to my right. I immediately slowed down and got into the same lane to get a good observation of this vehicle. There was little doubt in my mind that it was Felicia's minivan. Whenever she and I went anywhere we took it, rather than my car, and in fact she usually asked me to drive, so I knew that vehicle like it was my own. Any remaining doubts I had were entirely dispelled when I got a look at the plate number. It was Pyotr and Felicia all right.

Having detected Felicia's mini-van in time, my response to the situation was simple and quite anti-climactic. I did the obvious. Staying behind them, I got off the freeway at the next exit and made my way over to Westheimer and twenty miles of traffic lights and intersections until reaching my apartment. What was not anti-climactic was the nightmare going through my mind of what would have happened had I slid past Pyotr there, on the driver's side, and he had glanced over to see, not five feet from where he sat, my car going by. He knew my car too well. What would have happened to Felicia? What might he have done? Thank heavens it was only speculation, but it was the most unpleasant, disturbing speculation imaginable.

I never told Felicia about this narrow escape. She was always as anxious as I was about the possibility of Pyotr seeing my car and she was already doing all she could to insure this didn't happen. Telling her about what had occurred that evening would only have caused her further worry for no good reason. What I did instead was set out to trade my car in for another one, preferably ending up with Texas plates rather than having to transfer my own over. I had another reason, as well, to get a different car, and that was that my T-bird was beginning to use a lot of oil. I figured that either it was on its last legs or it needed some expensive repairs. It took some running around and a bit of persuasion, but I did succeed in trading it for a newer (and blander) Topaz. Thus was taken care of the last of the significant worries I had over some chance encounter between Pyotr and me. From this time onward, the likelihood of that had become extremely low, virtually nil.

Notwithstanding the described measures taken, Felicia never was able to get over the worry that Pyotr would learn that I was in Houston. Who could blame her? Any way you look at it, the outcome of that would be violence, against her, against me, against both of us, quite conceivably to the maximum degree. All the same, risk is inevitable in a relationship like that of ours. What were we to do? Go our separate ways? Neither of us wanted that. It was all a matter of choosing the best path, that which would get us where we wanted to go, yet offered the least risk along the way. About the only real argument I ever had with Felicia there in Houston was over this issue, what path we should be following.

Felicia dreaded the thought of Pyotr detecting my presence in Houston. Subsequently, she felt that it would be safer for Pyotr to know that I was "moving" there to be a student. Essentially, she wanted a return to the status quo of the previous year when I had been a "family friend" able to visit frequently. Such an arrangement would have certain undeniable benefits, no doubt; but, in place of the current, minimized risk that we were managing well enough, there would be a host of new risks to deal with. First and foremost would be the communicating to Pyotr of my enrollment at the university in Houston. Family friends do not transplant themselves two thousand miles to be near each other; only lovers do that. To my thinking, this risk alone was sufficient to nix the idea. But even getting past that, the potential of any of a thousand little missteps was a risk inherent in any direct interaction involving all three of us, Pyotr, Felicia and me. To my thinking, what Felicia was proposing here was about like leaping out of the frying pan into the fire. To say that I viewed such a proposal with disinclination would be an understatement.

The debate between Felicia and me over this matter had been ongoing for some time, since March, if not earlier; but it came to a head on the last day we got together before she left for an extended summer holiday to Poland. This was late May. Felicia wanted me to visit Pyotr while she was away — he would feel that I was visiting him that way, rather than suspecting that my visit was only for a chance to see her — and tell him that I had been accepted by the law school in Houston and would be taking up residence there in August.

I loved Felicia. I really did. And I wanted to do what she wished if only to calm her fears and make her happy. But I also really felt this was an unwise path to follow. We argued long and hard that day. We were at my apartment. At one point I told Felicia that I was already doing as much for her as I could and if this wasn't good enough then I might as well just pack my things and go. It was the plain truth too. Hearing that, she realized that she had been putting too much pressure on me and she apologized.

We kissed and made up, shedding some tears together, with her telling me that whatever I decided to do would be okay with her and me telling her that I would think it over some more.

So we said our goodbyes, heartfelt goodbyes, and Felicia left. After she was gone from my apartment that afternoon, I was in a bit of a quandary as to which of the two paths I should follow, hers or mine, and a real quandary as to which I would follow.

The last time I saw Felicia was that same evening towards ten. Her visit was a surprise for me and a real treat for us both. It was rare for us to meet outside of Pyotr's work hours. Felicia had gone alone to a wine and cheese at a museum and we had just a few minutes to share as she headed back home. When these treasured moments had passed — as they always do, in the blink of an eye — I jumped in her mini-van with her and rode to the edge of the city. Felicia and I had said goodbye to each other so many times before, and on so many of those occasions the foreboding of a tragic permanence to the goodbye had been so palpable (and all too possible), that you would think by this time we would have been inured to the pain, dismissive of the foreboding. We weren't. This goodbye wrenched us as much as any other, felt already just as eternal as the rest had threatened to be. Our parting could hardly have hit us harder had we known that this one would actually be forever.

Chapter 20

Fast-forward three and a half months now to the present and a very changed world. Yesterday, on the sixth, I blew into Calgary after a long, hard trip from a far city — no longer Houston — where I had been working for the past few weeks. Arriving in the morning, I wandered over to a park where I found a nice big warm rock in the sun to recline against and get some much-needed sleep. I had hardly slept in a week. I was so glad the sun always shines here.

Toward dusk I made my way to the south edge of the city and started walking. I walked down MacLeod and then hung a right at the Marquis of Lorne. From there it would be a simple matter of following my nose until I arrived here at Allen Bill Pond. What's that, twenty miles? Thirty? As if I cared! In the last two months or so I've walked more than in the last two years put together. The prospect of ten hours of trudging was nothing, especially with my journey's end all but in sight.

As it turned out, I didn't even have to walk most of that twenty or thirty miles. And this is testimony to what good people Albertans are. Truly good people. As I was traipsing along — traipsing, mind you, not hitch-hiking — first one vehicle, an old farmer, stopped and gave me a lift for a few miles until we hit his turn-off, and then another one, a cowboy this time, on his way to Cochrane, stopped and told me to hop in. Between the two of them, it was really only the last few miles left for me to walk.

Felicia, Felicia, Felicia...

I arrived here in the wee hours of the night, nothing but the stars to keep me company. The cool, fresh air was too cool, too fresh, for me to enjoy at rest — and I was too fatigued to remain active for no good reason, so I did what I could to pollute the cool, fresh air with a campfire beside which I curled up for a fitful little doze.

When dawn broke, I stirred myself and took a stroll around. I was struck by nostalgia, though nostalgia was not my purpose in coming here.

Why did I come to Allen Bill Pond? Why, indeed? I came to see Felicia. The month of June witnessed a drastic turn of events and I've been incommunicado ever since. No contact with family, no contact with friends, for sure none with my kochanie.

At daybreak, after getting a good look around, I picked this spot, a picnic table by the pond, and ensconced myself here. It's on a grassy bank across the water from the parking area and so it gives me a good view of the incoming traffic.

Dawn climbed through the morning to noon, and noon soared effortlessly over the land as the day progressed. People have come and gone. Picnickers, sport fishermen, hikers, lovers. But no Felicia. Discreet yet thorough, all day long I have inspected every new arrival, vehicle by vehicle, passenger by passenger.

Would Felicia come? There was no tryst to keep. We had arranged no rendezvous. Yet, if she wants to see me, as I know she does — as I well know, even without having been told by my lawyer (who refused to return her any message whatsoever from me) — then this is her chance. For today is our anniversary, our first anniversary. My kochanie knows me well enough to know where my thoughts would be on this day, and to know that neither hell nor high water could keep me from coming here to be with her.

The afternoon wore on. I began to wonder if I was expecting too much of Felicia...

No, my darling, the tables have turned: even as you are now out of danger, so I — ironically enough — am in it. I do not expect less of you than I do of myself, especially not in these reversed circumstances. If I could be here then you could be here too. You should be here with me...

171

Love is a funny thing, Reader. It's all about faith. If your faith in it is all-consuming, then so too can it, your love, be all-consuming. But if your faith in it wavers, so too will it waver; and if your faith in it dies, so too will it, your love, die.

As this day has drawn to a close, my amazement at Felicia's failure to appear has grown and grown. (Even as Myself-outside-myself has to smile in looking at myself and be amazed that I have the audacity to feel said amazement — and has also to wonder just how completely, utterly out of touch with reality I am.) I undertook this pilgrimage to Allen Bill Pond with an all-consuming faith in a love that too was all-consuming. Nothing else could have driven me to come. Not a waver in either — faith or love — did I feel all through the morning or in the first hours of the afternoon. But when mid-afternoon, the time I most expected my darling's arrival, had passed, I began to feel the stirrings of doubt.

I have now spent these twilight hours of our anniversary in reverie, thinking back over the last couple years, my life with Felicia. As faith is the immersion in a theory, so the disruption of faith is the subsequent re-emergence from the same, something similar to an awakening.

I loved Felicia. There is no doubting that. Yet my concept of love is unequivocal on the point of reciprocity. Love has to be equal and opposite. If it is not then it is just a mirage, a vanity, a flattery. I am beginning seriously to wonder if that was all this had been. Of course, in all fairness, there could also be any number of reasons making it impossible for Felicia to join me for our anniversary. I had thought a few days ago that I might not make it here in time myself...

Anyway, now that the sun has gone down, I know that tonight the stars will have me again all to themselves. So it's time to put my thoughts away. I will take the heart from my wallet, the one that says 'You are on the threshold of a lifetime of love', and lay it to rest on the gentle bosom that is the surface of this pond. Then I will set out back for my city, and another far city. It is, will soon be, too cold not to be walking.

And that, dear Reader, is that. End of story. Nothing more to tell.

Allen Bill Pond.

Works by Gary Wilson

Island (the one that wasn't supposed to be)

Gary's first novel, this story follows a young man overtaken by events who finds himself a fugitive fleeing from the law. Although a tale of action, it is in the interludes of thought that we see that this narrative serves as an analysis and criticism of existentialism.

Where Then O Bliss

A prequel to *Island (the one that wasn't supposed to be)*, this romance about the love between an idealistic student and a victim of severe spousal abuse serves as an analysis and criticism of romanticism.

The Deity of Life

A compilation of essays elucidating the philosophy that Gary has developed, bioism.

The Inframotionality Model

A physics model that is an alternative to the standard physics model and overcomes the structural defects of relativity.

Theophilus

An analysis of the eyewitness accounts of the life of Jesus which serves as an analysis and criticism of Christianity.

CA 2013

A vision of the greatness within Calgary's reach.

Please visit www.garywilson.ca to see more details and the most current listing of the works by Gary Wilson.

About the Author

Gary Wilson is a Canadian, born and raised in Calgary.

Having been witness to the vicious spousal abuse of a dear

friend in the mid-'90s, he found his life as a promising law

student taking a dire left turn when the authorities charged

him with the killing of her husband. In 2001 he was convicted

of homicide by a Texas court of law and sent to prison,

remaining there until 2006. Today he lives with his wife and

children in Calgary where he is a business owner.